WHEN ANGELS

LEAD YOU TO HEAVEN

TRANITA A. RANDOLPH

WHEN ANGELS LEAD YOU TO HEAVEN

Scripture quotations marked as NIV are taken from the New International Version of the Bible.

Scripture quotations marked as KJV are taken from the King James Version of the Bible.

Copyright © 2015 by Tranita A. Randolph

ISBN: 978-0-9970900-0-0

ACKNOWLEDGEMENTS

In the years of 1997 and 2000, I along with Rodney K. Nelson, Sr. were blessed with two boys, Rodney Keith Nelson, Jr. aka SugaPimp and Rodell Miles Nelson aka RadioRoc. This book was inspired by my journey with the boys.

There are so many people that have crossed our paths at some point or another since 1997 and I would like to acknowledge them. This list is not an exclusive list. If I were to make special mentions of each of you, I would be writing another book to properly thank you.

First, I would like to thank my oldest daughter, Tranisce Armstrong and her husband De'Von Armstrong for loving me unconditionally and having a listening ear over the years when I just needed to vent. You have blessed me with two beautiful grandchildren, Tranae and Aidan. To my youngest daughter, TraShawn Randolph, you have been my "ride or die" from day one. I could never express what it meant to me to just breathe while you tended to your brothers. Your beautiful babies, Trinity and Jaxsen always bring a smile to my face. To my family; my mother Corliss Hogan (RIP) who allowed me to be mouthy as a youth and unknowingly preparing me for the advocacy skills I would need for my boys later in life; my father, Leonard E. Randolph, Jr, (RIP) who showed me what it meant to pull yourself up and to never give up; my aunt, Gwen Randolph-Black who never turned her back on me. I love you from the bottom of my heart. To my uncle Kerry Black, who did not waiver in his strength as a man when it

3

was necessary to step up to the boys and handle their aggressions. My uncle Permus Hall, Jr., you were always there to ride shotgun with the boys and I around town when they needed calming down. To Brian Purnell, the young man who gave me the opportunity to call someone son before I even gave birth to your brothers, I thank you for your commitment in assisting me with both Rodney and Rodell in the early days of their youth. My godmother Cecelia Mayden; my surrogate aunts Minister Becky MaysJenkins (also my chief editor) and Callie Terrell, for continuing to be the picture of my mother's best friends in her absence. To the caregivers of the boys, Lamika Davis, you will forever be my beloved sister because of the love you showed both Rodney and Rodell; Clifford, Teresa and Nerissa Holden, thank you for inviting Roc into your home and loving him with your whole heart; Keisha Carrington, you always said that Rodney was "your son" and I believed you had that real motherly love for him, thank you. The remainder of my personal care attendants and respite providers, Bernie M., Pete and Tonia S., Gmasnoh N., Jonrell M., and Someko D. (RIP), it takes a village to raise a child and I'm honored that you were not only an intricate part of our village but our family. To the one and only Keisha S-D., you have been a terrific friend to me, as well as an aunt and wonderful caretaker to both SugaPimp and Roc. You already know what awaits you in heaven for the unconditional love you gave them. To my Charlotte, NC family, Mario B., Valencia S-K, Patricia W., Thelma R., Prophetess Velma H., Elder Shelby T., Adrienne B. and Nicole V., I thank each one of you for your prayers and support from day one. To the New Life Fellowship City of Praise Partakers, I thank you for ushering us into your hearts. To Pastor John P. Kee and First Lady Kee, thank you for encouraging me to bring my boys to church, regardless of what looks and stares we received. To my

4

Alexandria, VA family and friends who have shown unconditional love to us, you are greatly appreciated. My church family at Ebenezer Baptist to include Pastor Albert Jackson and First Lady Jackson, bless you for being obedient and embracing us in this short amount of time. To my closest friends Pam T. and Bernadette F., thank you for the many conversations over the years when you were there to just let me vent, cry or even just hold the phone and listen to me break down. You would sit with me and allow my boys, your nephews, to beat you up, hug and love on you. You will always have a special place in my heart. To the Wanzer and Miller families of Alexandria, VA, the Blacks, Ouzts and Adams/Owens families, I speak blessings over each of you for opening up your hearts and lives to Rodney, Rodell and myself. To each of you that watched from the sidelines and had no idea how to approach us to be a part of our lives, I pray that God's unconditional love finds you and wraps its' arms around you along your journeys.

To the wonderful medical staff at Levine Children's Hospital, (Charlotte, NC) you were always the epitome of southern hospitality coupled with medical professionalism, thank you. In addition, I would like to thank the medical staff of both the Pediatric and Intensive Care units at INOVA Fairfax Hospital (Falls Church, VA). It is because of you that I hold the bar high in my medical expectations. There has never been a physician that has allowed me to call her any time of the day or night other than Dr. Magdolna I. (RIP) (and Betsy L., her Physician's Assistant). You made yourselves available to me no matter what and I truly appreciate your dedication.

I would like to also acknowledge the teaching and administrative staff at Metro School in Charlotte, NC. The dedication they offered was greatly appreciated. While living in Alexandria, VA within the Fairfax County limits, Rodney and Rodell attended the Key Center and were educated by both teachers and paraprofessionals. I would like to thank them for their dedication toward ensuring that the boys' educational goals were achieved as closely as possible. Once Rodney entered into high school, he attended T.C. Williams High School in Alexandria, VA within the City of Alexandria jurisdiction. Here is where he was able to complete his education. At TCW we came across a staff that went above and beyond teaching. To speak on inclusiveness, these individuals eventually became a part of our family. To the teaching staff, paraprofessionals and students alike, I thank each one of you. Your dedication to Rodney's last year of school was remarkable. I would like to personally thank each of you that assisted in any capacity with his personal graduation ceremony which was held January 9, 2015. To Jacqueline E.M., Justine N., Gregory E. (SugaBear), Ronald L., Dawud R., Aster K., the paraprofessionals, aides, and administrative and support staff, I salute each of you as I say thank you. You all rock!

My current support system is strengthening me and has been consistent in what I need to help continue on. You are so very much needed and loved. To each one of my supporters that have taken the time to purchase this book, I thank you and pray that after reading about our journey, you will have a better understanding of God's faithfulness. Always remember that He is the same God today as He was yesterday and there is nothing too hard for you to endure as long as you lean and depend on Him. I will continue to follow Jesus and share my story in hopes that it blesses or encourages someone.

Again, I thank you and send blessings of love to all.

FOREWORD

This book was placed in my spirit a few years ago. The divine instruction to share my story had never been one that I set out to do on my own. There were several reasons pointing me in the direction of why I should venture into the world of writing. First, I have always had a gift of gab and would find myself at any given time talking to anyone who would listen (willingly or unwillingly) to me as I shared my journey with my boys. Secondly, but by far, no less important is my ability to testify and tell of God's goodness came natural. I felt it to be an honor to share my tests, which through time became my testimonies. Then of course, thirdly, there has always been that talent of being able to put together a sentence, paragraph, letter or even a resume that would sound as if it had been written professionally. However, I had never thought that the combination of the three things would lead me to this point.

After years of sharing bits and pieces of my assignment in life and all of the many ups, downs, trials, tribulations and victories, I'm here. It's been prophesied on several occasions that this is what God wants me to do. I received the prophetic word with open arms and great intent to fulfill it. Subsequently, several things got in the way. Me for one. Life. Hospital visits. Deaths. Me again. Ultimately, me.

I soon, realized that I needed to go to God on my own and seek His face and direction because I kept receiving the same word over and over again to "write the book". I did just that and if you have not figured it out by now, He gave me his thumbs up. I could see the pages of my life clearer than I ever had at that point.

There are so many avenues I could take this book. Even with as many medical issues I can share, I am not interested in making this a medical publishing. This is about my faith, my angels and of course, my trust in God.

So, I welcome you to take a brief walk with me. Along this walk you will find out that both my boys Rodney and Rodell were born with Alpha Thalassemia Retardation, X-linked (ATR-X[1]), a rare genetic disorder. So rare, that at the time of their diagnosis, in 2007 (they were the only African Americans), there were only 198 documented cases in the entire world. This diagnosis was found while we were living in Charlotte, NC and at the encouragement of a geneticist, there were several submissions to Duke University until there was finally a match to their personal medical and mental symptoms. Within the realm of ATR-X[2], there are a number of challenges that arise individually and collectively. In addition to the ATR-X syndrome, my boys had what the medical field called for a lack of better words, a double whammy, to also include a severe aggressive behavior or a defiance behavior.

---

[1] A newly defined X-linked mental retardation syndrome association with Alpha Thalassaemia.
J Med Genet 28, 729-733. *Gibbons RJ, Wilkie AOM, Weatherall DJ, Higgs DR. (1991)*
[2] Alpha Thalassaemia mental retardation, X-linked. Orphanet J. Rare Dis. 1:15. *Gibbons RJ (2006)*

Primary to having a diagnosis of any medical condition, any label of a physical disability, a documented level of intellect deficiency or even medication for any of these, there is one thing that always took precedence over everything. That one thing is the unconditional and everlasting love between a mother and her child(ren). The type of love that whether your child has a medical diagnosis or not, you as a mother will stand up for, advocate for and love them beyond words could ever explain. My prayer is that upon completion of this read, you will find yourself in a better place, mentally, emotionally and spiritually.

MY PRAYER

Father I stretch not just my hands, but my whole heart to
Thee.

No other help is greater than You.

Lord, as You decided to set a plan into place for my life,

You carefully hand-picked me oh God and for that I am
grateful.

I thank You for pruning me not just up until the beginning
of this journey oh Lord,

But I thank You for the continued pruning, the shaping, and
the shaking up.

Oh God, forever as the day is long, will I bless Your Holy
name.

For without You, oh God, I would not have been able to
make it through.

Without You Lord, we would have been counted out long
ago.

Father, you are my alpha and omega and it is Your say that
says "it is so."

I trust, believe and wait on You and Your direction, oh
God.

There is not a day that You will not allow my enemies to be
my footstool,

See the righteous forsaken or their children beg for food.

For this oh God, I honor and exalt Your name.

With this prayer, I humbly say Amen.

INTRODUCTION

When God puts together a plan for our lives, we are not included in the making of it. He decides, what we go through, when we go through it, how we endure each situation, how long it will take us to conquer or complete each trial and what the end result will be.

Initially, I thought the plan for my life was to sing. He blessed me with a voice with a 7-octave range that would be able to take me on a journey that I could not even begin to imagine. However, in the earlier years of my life, I opted to take a different route. Needless to say, it was a route that was not conducive to what He had planned for me. I didn't realize at the time that I was "planning" my own life. God decided that the gift that I was blessed with would be used in another fashion.

In telling my story I remind myself that my vocal gift of singing is being used to sing a new song. A song of advocacy for my children, Rodney and Rodell. Knowing and understanding this has given me the strength and faith that I needed to handle each and every task with them. I have only met a handful of individuals that can say, they have (had) a talent or ability and did not use it, yet they thank God that in the midst of their disobedience, God kept that talent only to allow them to use it in another way.

Knowing that God has kept you and your blessing for a specific reason is nothing short of a miracle. He loved me enough to preserve what would be needed in one of the most important tasks in my life. A journey that would allow me to speak up, talk about, and advocate for two special needs children that did not have a voice of their own. Each time I think about what He not only did for me, but for them and realize that He gave them a mother who could and would use her voice for them, there is only one word.....Hallelujah!

THE SOURCE

Have you ever wondered how someone seemed so happy? Why, when you know they have been going through some life changing events, they are able to promote positivity, smile or even encourage someone else who may not be doing so well?

How does that person hold up? Why have they not lost it? Shouldn't they have sat down in the middle of the grocery store and just cried? Maybe even scream at the top of their lungs because a parking space they were patiently waiting for was just snatched up by an uncaring and impatient driver?

What's holding them together? Are they made from something that you aren't made of? There has to be a reason for the ability to just stand strong and hold their head up the way they do. However, for the life of you, you just are not able to figure it out.

Well, they are different. Not a bad different. The kind of different that can only come from one source. A source that can see you through a bad relationship or a divorce. The same source that can allow you to find comfort like no other during the grieving process. It's just one word and it's the most powerful source that any of us could ever link ourselves to. That source is none other than God and His word that can get you through anything is faith.

Faith. What is faith?[3] "Now faith is the substance of things hoped for, the evidence of things not seen." Simply put, to believe even if you are not able to see it. Hope for a particular outcome and know that the end result will be okay.

So you mean to tell me that I'm supposed to believe in a source (God) that I cannot see and hope (faith) the expected outcome (evidence of things not seen) and know that all is well? Exactly. Now follow along and watch how a life of trials and tribulations along with a couple of angels can lead you to your faith.

---

[3] "Now faith is confidence in what we hope for and assurance about what we do not see." *Hebrews 11:1 (NIV)*

THE BEGINNING OF MY MIRACLES

It was almost as if I were planning a big party. One that would last for years. I was expecting a child, I wanted to celebrate, plan the big event, and arrange the day of delivery to my satisfaction. The announcements are made. I would blurt out with excitement to any and every one that would listen, "I'm having a baby"!! My pregnancy went on without any hitches and I arrived at the 37 week gestational stage. During my last doctor appointment, I realized that something was wrong. There was no fetal movement. After several attempts to jolt the fetus into movement, my physician decided to send me to the hospital with the instructions of monitoring fetal movement and if no change then a C-section would be my method of delivery.

After my admission into the hospital for monitoring, a few hours eventually turned into fifteen. At this point, my baby had stopped breathing and an emergency C-section was performed. Bells, whistles, buzzers and beeps all alarmed the medical professionals and myself that there was something truly wrong. I saw him briefly. He was blue. A blue that I had always heard of but never witnessed on any human being before. The medical staff worked diligently and resuscitated him as I was swiftly moved from the birthing area. Hours later I was told I had a son who was in the Neonatal Intensive Care Unit (NICU) however, he was doing fine. Fine? How can you be doing fine, yet be in an Intensive Care Unit? That was my question. I felt my whole world shake. I had confirmation even before I had the chance to see him. Yet the confirmation of what was to come allowed me to remain calm and clear-headed in order to fully understand what was expected of me as his mother.

Born at 6 lbs. 5 oz., and 20 inches in length, Rodney was of average birth weight and height. What was not average about him was his hypotonic or low muscle tone. He was floppy from birth. Due to the lack of oxygen during his delivery, it was evident to the physicians that he had suffered some brain damage. No one however, could tell me how much. Then, to all involved, came yet another surprise. He had also been born with a cleft of the soft palette. With this medical issue came feeding challenges. The soft palette was split in half (cleft). There was nothing at the roof of his mouth for his tongue to press up on. Thereby making it difficult to not only suck (breast or bottle), but the hole allowed all fluids to travel up through his sinus cavity and out of his nose. The only way for him to feed was through a Nasogastric (NG) tube.

There were many moments, days and weeks that his life seemed to others as bleak. Everyone offered their congratulations on his birth but those congratulatory statements were outweighed by "I'm so sorry he is sick". I didn't realize until years later that these comments could have been very detrimental to my outlook had I taken them in and accepted them. The months of traveling back and forth to visit him, sit with him, pray for him had not even touched what I now know to be my faith. I was on auto pilot and just doing what I was led to do. To trust and believe and know that this was supposed to be.

Once discharged from the hospital, I found myself in a brand new world. A world full of multiple visits to doctors, therapists, specialists, hospitals for more labs than I can count and the list would repeat itself all over again, weekly.

As he grew through infancy there were a few immediate challenges. As his inability to hold his formula down because of the severe Gastroesophageal Reflux Disease (GERD) resulted in no weight gain or medically speaking, failure to thrive. By the time he was six months old he was weighing less than when he was born. Again he faced more tests. At this point, medication to help with his Reflux were introduced, along with some speech therapy. This therapy at approximately nine months old was not to help him talk but to teach him to swallow.

Once he turned a whopping one year of age, he was having his first surgery. This procedure called "repair of the cleft of the soft palette" was to close the gap in his mouth. The surgeon at the initial consult informed me that I should expect to have this same procedure repeated several times throughout his youth due to the changing of the jaw line as he grows.

Surgery day comes and I do what I know what to do, I cry. I worry. I'm terrified because not only do I not know anything about taking care of this child, but with the "suggestion" that I prepare myself to have this procedure done several more times, I become a little uneasy about his future and his health. The surgery ended in success. Thankful for this outcome, I whisper a simple "Thank You Jesus."

Over the next couple of years as he grows and is able to eat chopped foods on his own, I focus on his other therapies. Physical therapy is introduced because his muscle tone has been seriously affected due to the lack of oxygen, and has left him unable to crawl, stand or walk. The two areas of physical and speech are coupled together and eventually occupational therapy is incorporated into the mix of things. So on any given day of the week one could find some sort of therapist in my home. If they were not at home with us, we were in their offices. These individuals, separately and collectively became a big part of my extended family. With the broad knowledge of their jobs and my willingness to learn, a bond formed that would be most beneficial for Rodney and his needs.

However, with every sunshine, there is a cloud that has the potential to darken the day. The one thing that never occurred to me was something that most of us take for granted each and every day. Without having the ability to walk, we have limited muscle tone to control our bowels. This of course, created an even bigger issue. Not being able to use the bathroom and have everything back up from the rooter to the tooter is a formula for disaster – fecal incompetence and intestinal pseudo-obstruction (the inability to have your waste pass through your intestines). Imagine knowing your child has not used the bathroom after many tries at over-the-counter medications, prescriptions and home remedies and you look up only to see it coming out of your child's mouth (yes, now we have added recurring vomiting). Scary is an understatement. So the ER visits start up again until an x-ray is done only to find out that there is not one open space in his entire intestinal tract for any waste to hide in. This of course starts a lifetime of more prescription meds and over the counter meds that work for a short time frame then stop for one main reason.....slow gastric motility.

If we didn't have enough medical issues and diagnosis, here comes yet another. Pneumonia. It didn't matter if it were bacterial or viral, he got it. Faithfully every six to eight weeks he was in the hospital for treatment. It appears that because of his GERD and his inability to swallow properly, we now have a breeding ground in his lungs for pneumonia.

Oh the things that are running through my mind at this point. My son, had been poked, prodded, looked at, flipped over, and turned around so many times by the age of two. My God, is all I can say. To see your child as sick as he was and you as a parent can do nothing to help him. I look around for anyone that can give me some answers, clarification, reasons, something. I listen to the doctors, nurses, specialists and understand (surprisingly enough), everything they are explaining to me. What I do not understand is why. Yet, I don't bother to ask. I accept it because there is always a calming existence in every situation that I have had to face with him. I just accept it "as is".

Then the day comes three years after the birth of my first son and I find out I am expecting another son. As most people have asked (as well as whispered amongst themselves), "why would you have another child if Rodney was born with those issues?" The answer is I did not know at that time that this was a genetic disorder. Also, families have been known for years to have one child out of their offspring to be somewhat different on many levels, however, it does not deter you from producing more children just because one child has challenges. If that were the case, then most parents who have had their first child to be either a cry baby, or end up being overly mischievous, don't generally take those issues into consideration when planning a family. Each of us is different, so why would I not believe that each of my children would be different.

The story begins again. Excitement, wanting to shout it to the masses, the whole nine yards. However, since I had an emergency delivery with my first son, my physician decided to avoid the possibility of having to do another emergency procedure, it was planned. Months later, it went as planned and I gave birth to a 7 lbs., 15 oz., 19-1/2 inch baby boy. All appeared to be well and there was no need for any NICU admission. He went home as planned along with me.

My oldest was finally walking at the age of three and able to say a few words which unfortunately were disappearing almost immediately. By the year's end, his entire vocabulary was lost as he entered into school. With him being in school, I of course had more time to spend with my youngest. I noticed that by the age of six months, he was having some issues. He cried constantly (not just your normal cry baby), but he cried when you touched him, and when you tried to stand him up on his legs. He was not able sit up on his own, and showed no interest in trying to hold his bottle. Red flags went up and I immediately placed the call to have him assessed for developmental delays. Mother's intuition was on target again. So, naturally the process of therapies started all over again. Whew! Was I tired yet? I don't believe I was. What I didn't know was that these two angels were a blessing. A blessing to not only me, but a world of others known and unknown. Again, I just accepted and marched on with my "as is".

Through the years the boys and I found ourselves frequenting many doctors. There was of course, their primary care physician, a neurologist for their aggressive behaviors, a developmental pediatrician, a neurologist whose specialty was rare neurological disorders, a gastroenterologist, and a geneticist.

On any given day there were a minimum of two medications per doctor for each child (adding up to approximately 10-12 medications each child). The task gets a tad bit trickier right here. I have two boys who have very low muscle tone in their mouths and I need to get them to swallow their pills. Then you add in their aggressive behaviors and attempting to dispense their medications can be adventurous. I can do nothing but laugh at this point when I think back to some of the moments of my daily routine.

Imagine a six and three year old who cannot swallow well, have the strength of grown men when provoked and are not interested in or willing to take medications. You got it, a big fight daily. I would try and disguise the medications in oatmeal, applesauce, or juice. Sounds easy right? Not hardly. Even though the boys were diagnosed with severe Intellectual Disabilities and moderate Intellectual Disabilities respectively, they were by far no dummies. They knew when it was time for medication and that I had put it in their food.

I could hold them down, sit on them, hit them with the sneak attack or at times, if someone was around, I could double team them. It didn't matter, on most days, I would be cleaning up from the floor whatever substance or concoction the medication was in. A victory would be not just getting the medication in, but getting it in without being bit, scratched, kicked, or even knocked in the head by them.

Medications were being prescribed in all forms. If I had liquids, I had to try and disguise it in their sippee cups with Gatorade (their drink of choice) or apple juice. On a number of days that was a relatively easy thing to do. However, on any other day, I may give them something mixed in with their drink(s) and the next thing I know I would hear the sipping sound then a second or two later, the cup would be seen flying across the room as if to say "get this mess outta here" and that was that. I could try and encourage, bribe, or even force them to drink in order to get it in them and you guessed it, there was a fight of the wills (with usually theirs winning).

Then there were the multiple attempts at dispensing the tablet form of meds. For a good while I found a really good method. This is where the oatmeal and applesauce would come in respectively. I could take all the pills ahead of time and fold them over into one of the bowls until the pill(s) would dissolve then feed it to them. Okay, this was a win-win situation here. Well, for a while anyway. Either the tablets came with an unpleasant taste that would overpower either of the foods used or again, they caught on to what I was doing. Once they caught on to what I was doing, there was absolutely no getting around it. I couldn't fool these little boys no matter how much I tried to pull the wool over their eyes.

So the next move was what? I had to find a way to be able to get all of their medication in them in a safe and accurate matter. This may seem like a no-brainer. However, the things that most of us find second nature or really simple, for me came with multiple challenges. Albeit, there was never a challenge that was too hard for God to see me or us through or to provide an avenue for success. As my frustrations grew in trying to handle even the simplest of things such as administering the medications, my faith and trust in the only one, God, grew, because I knew He would make a way for me to do it.[4]

On one occasion I was walking around in a pharmacy (waiting for a prescription to be filled) and a small voice (the Holy Spirit) says go find a pill crusher. I did and took it home, placed the crushed medicines in flavored yogurt and it was a tremendous hit for 10 years. At least up until all of Rodney's medications had to be crushed, dissolved and then dispensed through his feeding tube. We will get into that later in the book.

In speaking of their aggressive behaviors, it's a story all in itself. However, keeping it as brief as possible, I will share just a smidgen of it. During the timeframe when both boys were under the age of ten, family gatherings, outdoor events and general socializing always found us in some type of struggle. Imagine going to a birthday party on a Saturday afternoon at a facility built for children's fun. The facility has lots of children with parents, along with every type of noise to include bells ringing, children screaming, babies crying, music playing and oversized mascots walking around trying to greet the guests. This environment as fun as it may sound was a breeding ground for an outburst from at least one, if not both boys. If Rodney would get over stimulated from the environment he could be found at any time swiping everyone's pizza plates and drinks off the table top with one quick move of his arm. This activity would surely get everyone involved in the cleanup and one or two would try to aid me in calming him down. But that's not how the story ends. While Rodney is being tended to, then Rodell, would perceive the situation as a hostile situation for

---

[4] "See I am doing a new thing. Now it springs up; do you not perceive it? I am making a way in the wilderness and streams in the wasteland." *Isaiah 43:19 (NIV)*

his older brother and like most siblings, he would come to his rescue and attempt to attack one of us because he sensed we were hurting his brother, his ally, his partner in crime, so to speak. Chuckles and laughter surely come to the forefront now as I reminisce over it all. However, it was by the grace of God, that the many instances that were endured over the years, we all for the most part were able to remain safe. [5]

Safe is really not a good word to describe the above. Let's just say we survived. There were also many instances as they grew and I realized I had to pick and choose our outings. We missed out on quite a few. Then there were other occasions that the boys would decide that they were no longer best buds, comrades, or two peas in a pod. For any unforeseen reason their aggressive behavior could be turned on one another. Now you want to talk about a trying time?

---

[5] *"To him who is able to keep you from stumbling and to present you before his glorious presence without fault and with great joy" Jude 1:24 (NIV)*

RODNEY'S MEDICAL

I am going to backtrack for a moment in order to refresh yor memory and to provide more detail. Now Rodney, being my more medically-fragile son, has proven to be a true warrior since the day he came into this world. His life has been the picture of what it means to have strength and to push through until it gets better.

I was at what I believed to be a routine 37 week gestational appointment. During the appointment and examination there were questions asked and answered about my baby's movement and activity level that was not pleasing to my attending doctor. After explaining to him that I had not felt much movement for the last 24 hours, I was given all kinds of sugary treats to get what I considered to be a lazy sleeping little baby boy a rush to do what he was supposed to....kick me. It didn't work. The next step was to use amperage or to jolt him into moving. After several attempts of buzzing my belly a decision was made to send me to the hospital for observation with a plan of performing a caesarean section if there were no changes after an hour or two. However, that hour or two eventually turned into 15 hours with no improvement. At this point, my baby boy was found to be in trouble. He was suffering from a decreased heart rate due to the cord being wrapped around his neck. The next thing (yep you guessed it) an emergency C-section.

At birth he was asphyxiated and had to be resuscitated. The moment I saw him, even being under anesthesia, I knew something was not right. He wasn't crying, he was blue, a real blue, not a taint of the color. He was what they call hypotonic or "floppy baby syndrome". His poor little arms and legs were just like a little rag doll. This meant at this point the staff knew he had loss lots of oxygen. They were able to jump start him and his little lifeless body and it worked, there was a faint whimper. The signs of life….his life.

As I lay there listening to the hustle and bustle of everyone in the room, I could faintly hear orders being spewed out at every direction, to me it was total chaos. I could hear one of the doctors screaming for his Appearance, Pulse, Grimace, Activity, and Respiration (APGAR). Later I found out that each newborn is tested on these scores to assess them immediately after birth. The test is performed at the one and five minute marks after birth. On average, a scoring of seven and above is normal, scores ranging from four to six fall within the fairly low category and respectively, three and below are considered critically low.

At the one minute mark of Rodney's birth, his APGAR score was one. He was barely there and just holding on and fighting at the mere second he joined us here on earth. Bells, whistle, machines, footsteps, screaming voices were all a raging blur to me. By the time the five minute mark arrived, the attending medical staff was able to assess him with an APGAR score of four. Still being considered fairly low, this was by no means near the acceptable scoring of eight (where he would have been under normal circumstances). The staff continued to work on both of us and by the time I heard the ten minute declaration of his APGAR score of six, tears streamed down the side of my face as I mumbled "help me Jesus." As I drifted off into a medically induced slumber, I heard someone say "poor cutie patootie is going to be developmentally delayed."

The next thing I remembered hours later, was a nurse saying to me, "he is such a cutie pie, but I'm sorry, he is in our Neonatal Intensive Care Unit (NICU) and we will not be able to bring him to you. Let me know when you are ready and we can wheel you in to see your precious boy."

Naturally, I got cleaned up and re-gowned as quickly as my sore body would allow me to do so. I was ever so anxious to see him, touch him, and smell him. To my surprise, I was wheeled into another world. A world filled with questions, new language, unknown terms yet plenty of faith. That Hebrew 11:1[6] faith. That type where you can't see the outcome, yet, you know this is not it. There is more to come and it will be better.

The very first time I was able to truly able to lay my eyes on my newborn son, I of course did what any other mother would do, I smiled. I saw the machines, the incubator, the tube going down his nose passing his throat to his stomach, the IV lines with multiple bags hanging on the pole, the oxygen and of course the tube going into the top of his head. Yet, all I could do was smile. I saw a beautiful boy. To me, he was healthy. He was created to be what I later termed as "his healthy". It was at this point that the word "faith" clicked. If I could look into my few hours old newborn with all he had going on and still think about faith, I had already subconsciously began my spiritual road to being able to handle everything that God entrusted to me without me even knowing it.

---

[6] "Now faith is confidence in what we hope for and assurance about what we do not see." *Hebrews 11:1 (NIV)*

28

As the nurse started to leave me alone with my new miracle, I stopped her and asked, "How much does he weigh?" She replied with a smile, "He is 6 lbs. 5 oz. and 19-1/2" in length." I was relieved and let out a sigh. If I didn't know anything else, I knew that he was not underweight and that was a plus on his side. With everything else I saw, I found relief that at least he didn't have to fight because he was underweight, or so I thought.

At this point, the nurse returns and informs me that the house pediatrician and a neurologist would like to meet with me in order to explain to me what was going on with my son. At some point, during this first visit with him, my adrenaline, faith and maternal instincts all kicked in at once. I immediately took charge of the situation the best I knew how and agreed. I told her "that's fine. Please let them know I will be waiting in my room in about 30 minutes and they can join me there." I turned my attention back to Rodney and just looked, talked to him ever so quietly, telling him, "hey there little boy, I'm here and everything is going to be alright; we will get through this."

Once in my room, the two physicians met with me to provide some insight on what I would be faced with in the future. I was told of course, that the umbilical cord had been wrapped around Rodney's neck and he lost oxygen. They went on to explain the differences in losing small amounts of oxygen to being oxygen-deprived for longer amounts of time and the possible affects it could have on him. The possibility of having cerebral palsy, the inability to speak, being immobile, possibly wheelchair bound, or perhaps a mild to a profound deficiency in his intellect. There was so much to take in that at one point I thought my head was spinning. However, I continued to do the only thing I could do at that time. I sat there listening intently trying to keep a clear head in order to get a good understanding of what I was hearing.

After I listened to the possible scenarios about what the loss of oxygen could impose on my child's life, I realize that the ICU pediatrician is switching gears as if he has something else to tell me. I turn all of my attention from the neurologist to the pediatrician and just stared. I heard him say something but wasn't quite sure what he said, so my response was "excuse me?" He took a deep breath and said, "Your son was also born with a "clef of the soft palate (Cleft Palate - Topic Overview, 2014)". I looked at him bewildered and remember scrunching my nose up and saying, "Huh? What is that?" As they explained to me what a cleft of the soft palate is, (a cleft can be of either the hard or soft palate, both or the lip), I thought I felt myself falling to the floor. Although I didn't. However it wasn't any doing of my own[7]. It was God holding me, preparing me for the work He had predestined for me to do.

At this point, the questions came pouring out (finally). Of course I started with the simplest ones. "How can we find out about whether or not he has cerebral palsy?" Their response was "he does not appear to have any type of genetic disorder from our initial assessment, the diagnosing will be from monitoring the development of his brain over the next two years or so. We will also keep a close watch and test his motor skills. We will perform a CT scan of his brain for any abnormalities, and will proceed from there depending on the results." I understood that, so of course my next question

---

[7] "But He said to me, "My grace is sufficient for you, for my power is made perfect in weakness. Therefore I will boast all the more gladly about my weaknesses, in insults, in hardships, in persecutions, in difficulties. For when I am weak, then I am strong." *2 Corinthians 12:9-10 (NIV)*

was about the cleft. "How is this going to affect him?" The physicians then explained to me that because the roof of his mouth was not formed together that he would have a difficult time with feeding. I was asked whether or not I had planned on breast or bottle feeding. I informed them I had intentions of breast feeding. It was then explained to me that with any type of feeding he would have a difficult time latching on to breast or bottle, however, their Lactation and Dietician staff would definitely be able to assist me with it. For the time being, he was going to be fed via a nasogastric (NG) tube that had already been placed through his nose into his stomach. Rodney could be fed in this manner until a more beneficial way could be determined. They opted to go this route because of the cleft, everything that he would attempt to drink orally would more than likely come up through his nose since there was the large opening. Imagine the time you drank something and then during a laugh the liquid came back up to your nose. Well, this is what would have occurred if he had been allowed to feed from either the breast or bottle. The doctors explained to me that since I was planning to breast feed, that their staff would provide me with the information on providing my breast milk for him and bringing it to the hospital. I thought to myself, 'Oh yeah that's right, because my baby is not going home right now'. Reality started to set in.

Imagine planning for the birth of your new baby. You have a healthy pregnancy with no warning signs throughout of anything being different. Then all of a sudden your baby is here and everything you planned, everything you imagined for this time stops. Comes to a screeching halt. What do you do? What can you do? Do you allow yourself the opportunity to feel those raw emotions that have been stifled since this all began? Of course you do. Just not at that moment. At least that's what I told myself. This wasn't the time to sit around and mope because things had not turned

31

out the way that I had expected them. There would be more than ample time to cry, scream, or even throw something. So with that same attitude, I moved forward. How could I not move forward to my next? My son's very life depended on my movement, as well as mine.

After my discharge, I went into auto pilot mode. I knew that no matter what, I needed to show up in a big way in order for him to be in a position that would be most beneficial to him. So from that moment on, my movements, my conversations, my daily living, my attitude but most importantly my faith changed. It didn't matter that I had just had major surgery, I drove myself back and forth to that hospital sometimes twice a day to sit, watch, love, pray and trust God.

During the first few months, I talked to any medical staff that would allow me to stop them and ask questions. The internet became one of my best teaching tools because if there was something being discussed, I wanted to know about it as well as any and all options that would be available to us.

By the time Rodney was discharged, there had been many changes to his feeding schedules and the types of feeds he could handle. There were so many concoctions from breast milk, to breast milk with formula, to formula, to formula mixed with cereal and this was all before he was three months of age. Not only were we having a time trying to find a formula or even a built up formula that would be heavy enough to stay down. He had also been diagnosed early with gastroesophageal reflux disease (GERD) which kept his formula from staying down. With the cleft palate condition we turned to trying to feed him using different over-the-counter nipples. Because of the opening in his mouth he was unable to effectively use his tongue to provide a strong enough suck on a nipple.

However difficult things may appear to most at the start of his life, to me (and my auto pilot), it had already become second nature. The day finally comes when he is going home. We leave the hospital with baby boy, bags, prescriptions, special formula, lots of instructions, copies of tests, and of course referrals for several specialists. Was it overwhelming? Yes. Was I nervous? Absolutely. Those emotions were natural. Yet, even in all of the newness of everything, I still felt a calm sense over me.

As time moves on, there's a sense of a routine coming into play. Just as you do with an atypical newborn, I made adjustments to fit his needs and each day became a little easier. That was until I started noticing a change over the next few months. I started to notice he wasn't growing. I don't mean growing in the sense of he was just a small child or growing at a slower rate. I noticed that instead of gaining weight, Rodney was losing. He was losing enough weight to leave me a little concerned. So naturally, off to the pediatrician I go to see what is going on. Now, if you remember he weighed in 6 lbs. 5 oz. at birth and now at least six months later, the pediatrician weighs him and my son is now 5 lbs. 3 oz. He had lost weight which most newborns do, however, according to the pediatrician, that weight loss should have been during the time frame he was in the NICU and not at this moment. Upon completion of her assessment and a few labs, I was informed that she was diagnosing him with "failure to thrive". So unfortunately, he is admitted back to the hospital for extensive testing to determine exactly what was going on with him. However, he is not admitted to the NICU, he goes to the Pediatric Intensive Care Unit (PICU). Even though he was still a very young infant, I learned that once an infant is discharged from the hospital (even though he came from NICU) he is then considered a pediatric patient and therefore goes to another unit.

So now this is where the tears begin to flow, as I realize that I have to take my son to the hospital. As the day moves on and I am speaking to all of the attending medical staff and he has gotten situated in his room, a nurse comes to me and informs me that I have about 30 minutes left for visitation. It was not until that very moment that I realized that I would not be able to stay there with my son during this hospital admission. Reality sets in again. I knew he was going to be in the hospital and I had expected to be able to stay with him. However, what I did not take into consideration was the fact that this was an ICU admission again. Therefore, no parent overnight stays, at least not in this unit.

I muster up the strength and courage to lean over to him as he sleeps and say a little prayer again. In this prayer, I do not make it about the "Lord, can you....", or "Jesus turn this….." my prayer was simply, "Thy will be done…Amen." It was at that very moment that I accepted that no matter what I wanted, desired or sought after, my thoughts and expectations had to be lined up with the will of God.

Throughout this hospital admission and many others over the years, there was always a reason for me to hang my head and have some sort of pity party. However, I decided not to do that a long time ago. It's kind of akin to the theory of if you want better then you have to do better. The only way I knew how to make our life better was to do better. A better prayer life was the first thing on my agenda without me even planning for it. You see, God will allow certain situations to take place in our lives just so He can get our attention. Just because He allows us to go through something that changes our lives does not mean that we did something wrong in the past. It could very well be that He wants us to stay close to Him. He knows that if we don't have that solidified relationship we could be doing just the opposite of staying close to Him.

It is for this very reason that I thank and bless Him through all of the years that I have been raising the boys. Let me explain this as it pertains to my life and my obedience. I gave birth to two beautiful girls (Tranisce and Trashawn), as a teenager/young adult. I was fortunate enough to never have any major problems out of either of them, and I thank God for them. However, it was only God's grace and mercy that I was able to mature into the person that I would need to be before I was blessed with some real "motherhood tasks". I often share my testimony of how I was a teen parent, yet God loved me enough to wait for the right time to loan me the boys. He gave them to me when I was older, wiser and more mature. There would have been no way I would have been able to handle all of their medical, psychological and physical challenges if the births of the girls and boys would have been switched. I more than likely would have followed others' advice when they suggested in the boys' early years that I "place them somewhere" because it was too much for one person to handle on their own. So with that thought process, I have always tried to remain humble in knowing that I was carefully handpicked to raise two special needs children. In addition to remaining humble, I had to learn to remain thankful in spite of what my circumstances appeared to be. It was nothing but the hand of God that has kept me in my right mind and health in order to receive and carry out the assignment that He blessed me with.

RODELL'S MEDICAL

Now looking at all of the medical issues that we have encountered with Rodney, I find myself practically at the other end of the spectrum with Rodell. Three years later, my second son was born at a nice healthy weight of 7 lbs. 15 oz. and was 19-1/2" in length. He was a planned C-section due to my age (37 at the time) as well as the problems that arose during Rodney's delivery. My attending physician just did not want to take any unnecessary chances. Upon giving birth, Rodell was assessed after delivery as well as in the nursery only to find that everything was all within normal limits.

Moving along through infancy, I began to notice that he would cry a lot. Well, actually, he would scream, not just cry. I figured of course, as most mothers do initially, oh my, I have a real cry baby here. He was forever wanting to be held, coddled or just plain old be near (or up under) me and a few select others. I knew early on that this little one was going to definitely end up being what my grandma used to call "a hip baby". However, by the time he was in the 4-6 month range, I started to take notice that he was not showing any interest in lifting his head during tummy time, had very little interest in reaching and/or pulling for bright toys as well as a few other missed milestones. Needless to say, since I had been through a great deal of developmental delays and missed milestones with Rodney, I was a bit more in tuned with what should or should not be going on. In hindsight, I believe I spent a great amount of days holding my breath and waiting for something "different" to happen. Something in the "normal" scheme of things. Praying that this was not happening again. That history was not repeating itself, acknowledging to myself that this scenario was something I could seriously do without. However, this was not what was meant to be. At least a part of history would in fact, repeat itself.

By the time, Rodell was six months old, I decided to reach out to the local early intervention unit in my city. Even though this was one of the last things that any parent wants to do again, I eventually welcomed the assessment with open arms. I knew just from the short time that he had been living that there were at least two advantages at this point. The first advantage was, I had been through this with Rodney so I was more aware, and not inept about developmental delays. Once assessed, it was so much easier to request the various therapies he needed to get him a good jump start on his life skills.

Unbeknownst to me at the time, this little guy was a fighter, to say the least. He was able to blossom and catch on to many things rather quickly. Once he realized that no matter how much he cried, he participated in his therapy sessions, just to get it done. He showed an attitude of "okay I'm going to do it this time....now I've done it so leave me alone."

Once he was introduced to speech therapy which also included eating foods, he was ever so cooperative. He was so cooperative in this therapy that his first nickname came into play describing who and what his little body had become....Tubby.

My little or not so little Tubby started pulling, pushing, and knocking over any and everything he could maneuver with his little hands. On most occasions the object of his strength would be his older brother, Rodney. I'm not sure if he realized it at an early age of three (when he started walking) or if he just had that type of personality, but he acted as if he were the big brother. This was a far cry from the little round boy who in the early part of his toddler years, would just sit on the floor and cry. Cry to be picked up or cry just because you would not look at him. He would cry because his brother would waddle pass him and smack him on the top of his head and waddle on away laughing. (Yes they had many moments as atypical brothers do). However, those crying spells came to a screeching halt once he found his legs and was able to get around on his own.

It appeared at the time (and still did for years after), that once Rodell was able to walk, it was inevitable for him to share in the brotherly love that his older sibling had been giving to him the previous years. In other words, for every hit, punch or smack that he received prior to walking, he seemed like he was on a mission to return them all to Rodney. He began to follow him around and give him the business, just like all little brothers have done for hundreds of years.

This newfound love/hate relationship that Rodell helped to create seemed to spark an aggressiveness in both boys. The older he got the more aggressive he became. This character trait at times was as you could imagine very dangerous and could easily wear you out.

Safe is really not a good word to describe the above. Let's just say we survived. There were also many instances as they grew and I realized I had to pick and choose our outings. We missed out on quite a few. Then there were other occasions that the boys would decide that they were no longer best buds, comrades, or two peas in a pod. For any unforeseen reason their aggressive behavior could be turned on one another. Now you want to talk about a trying time?

As I am thinking back on the many individual and group fights that we have had, I can't help but remember one between Rodell and myself. We were in Charlotte, NC and he was about 11 years old and about 95 pounds or so. We were visiting someone and he was not happy because he wanted to go to one of his favorite corner stores. As I am sitting in the car he begins to kick and scream and bang his head on the back window. I immediately get out of the car and walk around to the back of the car to try and calm him down. He was not having it. He proceeds to grabs me and attempt to bite my hands, arms, or whatever he could get hold of. This went on for several minutes and I'm getting pretty frustrated and hot (because it's summer and we are down south) and the temperature is well above 85 degrees. So I decide to make an "executive" decision at this point to try and diffuse the situation. I take his seat belt off and offer him to get out of the car to take a walk to calm down. It begins to work, up until the moment I realize he does not want to turn back to go toward the car. I offer what I feel is a compromise of getting in the car in order to go to the store. This was not good enough for him. I suppose he felt since I did not want to take him to the store at first that he would get to the store on his own. Well the fight started all over again. This went on for what seemed like an eternity but was more than likely only 15 minutes at the most. He and I tussled back and forth, with sweat pouring off the both of us and neither of us wanting to be the one to give in and lose this battle. Just when I had him settled on the ground in a sitting position (or so I thought), and was thinking I had him calmed, he propels himself from the ground at the same time screaming and coming for my face. It was unbelievable. I saw strength, anger and determination in my son, all at the same time. Unfortunately, I had to keep him and myself safe, so I had to, for the lack of a better word, floor him. After we were settled, calmed, cooled off, and he was looking up at me with those beautiful eyes wiping his tears away and saying "mama, luh luh (love you), I could do nothing but put my anger and frustration away and give him a big bear hug and tell him that I loved him too. This was the end result of one of many violent outbursts. Of course, as our visit ended I took him to the corner store so he could get what he wanted, his favorite pink lemonade drink and powdered donuts. No I did not reward his behavior. I rewarded his ability to realize in the midst of his intellectual disability and his inability to control his psychotic outbursts that he was wrong and his ability to acknowledge it and apologize for his behavior.

There were several times during the years that I found myself in dire straits concerning our living arrangements. Being a single parent of two special needs children, I was unable to work most of the time. Now don't get me wrong, I never used them or the life that God blessed me with as a crutch. However, most days it was just too much on one person to go through the motions of anything that was close to a "normal life with atypical children".

Most days, I longed to be in the workforce alongside my peers, using the level of intelligence that I was blessed with in any avenue of work. There were many times that I would push through my challenges[8] and apply for positions that I knew I would easily be offered. I would, of course accept offered positions only to be faced with the obstacle of dealing with some sort of medical emergency from my son, Rodney. Now I'm not talking about just a trip to the ER type of emergency, I'm referring to an admission to the hospital with the usual intensive care unit type of emergency. Of course, with any of the life threatening scenarios he faced

---

[8] "For I know the plans I have for you," declares the Lord, "plans to prosper you and not to harm you, plans to give you hope and a future." *Jeremiah 29:11 (NIV)*

(from gastrointestinal to seizures to name a few), my presence as a parent was absolutely necessary.

Leaving a child in the hospital who was very sick, unable to communicate his wants and needs, as well as who had extremely aggressive behaviors (that warranted the use of soft restraints), was just not something that in my opinion a good parent did.

So instead of going to work, I opted to be a stay at home mother with the both of them. Especially since most of his life, Rodney was being admitted to the hospital at least every six to eight weeks on a regular basis. Most times these hospital admissions lasted a minimum of 1-2 weeks to the longest being almost 4 months.

Between running back and forth from the hospitals to sit with Rodney and meeting with doctors, specialist and therapists to driving Rodell to and from school, there was not enough time to think about working. As the years went by I realized that living with various individuals in the area where we were from, was not going to be the end all to everything for us.

You are probably asking why I didn't just share a place with someone who could or would help us. Well the answer is simple.....we tried. It was just too difficult. Imagine two little boys living in your household. Well, not just two little boys but two little boys who were loud, rambunctious, fighters of one another (and anyone who dared to step in between them), not understanding the do's and dont's of safety and security and/or personal space. Let's just say it gets somewhat old when you have to keep apologizing for the broken this or that or the scratches or bruises caused by them on someone else.

So the morning came during the Spring of 2005, after getting the boys off to school, I found myself with a direction that was dropped in my spirit to go to Charlotte, NC. I had never been there so of course there was a little bit of confusion that came with this. However, when God gives you a direction you learn to not second guess but to just do it. So I was obedient and went on the internet to do some research about Charlotte, NC. I made some calls about rental properties that were within my budget and quickly made plans to visit. In the next two weeks I found myself traveling alone to Charlotte down 85 South, a road I had never been down, much less heard of. I drove around for a while throughout that weekend (getting lost even with mapped out directions), finding the various properties. After a meeting with one of the property managers and explaining my situation of being a single parent with two special needs children and unable to work and living in the Northern Virginia area, she assured me that she could and would help me. Well, by the time my weekend was winding down, I received a phone call informing me I had been approved and would I be able to move within the next 3 weeks. So overjoyed with this, I journeyed back to VA thinking about the plans I needed to put into place in order to make this happen. Fast forward to the move in date, my family and I along with my belongings traveled back down to North Carolina and the boys and myself became Charlotteans.

As you know, when life's challenges are resolved, there's always another coming right behind it. Now I am in a strange city with two boys with multiple disabilities in the summer (school had already let out) and no real plans keeping occupied. Oh boy was I in for a treat.

First things first was to get linked up with physicians, therapists and case management agencies. One day that will forever be in the corner of my mind and heart, is the day I decided to make a call to set up an appointment to have them assessed for services. I was on the phone with a social worker at the local mental health agency. We were going over their detailed history in order to determine where to start with their services. However, as my normal life at the time would have it, the boys kept interrupting our conversation by fighting. I had to keep asking the worker to hold on so I could attend to them. I would stop to say "stop it".

The conversation would pick back up then I would stop to say "don't hit your brother" and then I would continue. Again I would stop and say, "behave.....noooo.....don't hit him.....stop biting me.....sit right here, you sit over here." Then taking a deep breath would attempt to start the conversation again. Once a few more questions were asked I found the boys were up and at it again, this time circling me swinging at one another, screaming at one another, biting one another, scratching one another, and anything else. I am in the middle with the phone (finally throwing it on the floor) to grab and separate the two of them only to find them turning on me. Yes, you heard right. It was at that point I was at a disadvantage because I was being jumped and ganged up on by two little boys.

You are probably laughing and saying that I didn't have any control over my boys. Actually, it was just the opposite. We all have encountered someone (man, woman or child) at some point in our lives that was behaviorally or emotionally challenged and we want to spank, chastise or even punish them but realize that no matter what we do, it doesn't help. They seem to be apologetic at that point in time yet, a few minutes later that same behavior reappears just as if it was never addressed previously. Imagine dealing with that in your daily life, from two individuals that as they got older I realized they could be found "feeding off one another" and their aggressions.

There were times when they would fight and I would choose not to intervene. I would watch to ensure that neither of them got seriously hurt in the beginning. Some people would ask me why I would allow them to fight and I would simply say "they are brothers and regardless of their disability they still need to learn what it means to love someone enough to want to go to the ends of the earth for them" (and as it stands at this point; that is exactly what they did). So the end result of their battles I would grab them and explain to each the do's and don'ts and how they have hurt each other and make them apologize by hugging and giving kisses. They may not have been able to express themselves as eloquently as we are capable of doing, but in their own expressive beings, their apologies were offered, the love was given and received. The end of this ongoing lesson in the early years resulted in their ability to love one another enough to love and protect each other under any and all circumstances. Hence, the day (one of many) I attempted to break up their fight(s) would end in them turning on me but yet protecting one another from someone other than their brother.

To continue speaking on the incident of trying to set up the assessment for help with Rodney and Rodell. The hardest part of the whole day was picking up the phone to make that initial call. I had to ask for help and admit that things I found myself dealing with were unfamiliar to me and a bit overwhelming.

After I get the boys separated and I pick the telephone from off the floor, I say (very much out of breath) "hello....I'm back." I can hear the social worker saying "my God....help her. Ma'am, are you there?" I state that I am and begin to form another sentence as the social worker says "you have a lot on your hands and you need some help. Can I send help for you? You stated you don't sleep and I can only imagine how frustrating it is with both boys." Again she asked, (as my infamous "DoubleTrouble" start up the fighting), "ma'am, would you please allow me to send you some help?" Now keeping in mind I was a very pride filled person then however, I agreed and said "yes, please." It was at that very point I truly understood all that I had been doing and going through and the emotions just started pouring out of me. The tears from my strength allowed my heart to open up in order to receive the real blessings of having two special needs boys.

RODELL'S YOUTH

Rodell's medical conditions were not as severe as his brother's. He was a healthy baby and had an appetite to match his size. His growth spurts were just that. Nothing tremendous, at the same, not so little to cause concern.

He transitioned from breast to bottle relatively easy and then happily moved to cereal. The issue when it was time for him to start eating cereal from a spoon as opposed to the bottle was the low muscle tone he had in his face. Think about how a baby who is being introduced to cereal and/or baby food and how he/she is reluctant to taste or swallow what has been placed in their mouth. This part of feeding was the same for him although it was a little more intense because he wasn't able to swallow. During those first rare moments of being able to get the food in his mouth, he would gag and choke because he was not able to allow the food pass his tongue. This was a very trying experience. I had a child who had a healthy appetite yet was not able to swallow the food he was being fed. This is where the speech/language therapies came into play. When you hear speech therapy mostly you think of teaching someone how to talk. What I learned was that it is not limited to just that. The same muscles we use to form our words are the same muscles we use to eat.

With intense speech therapy set into place, it was just a matter of time before he got the hang of the full process of eating. It didn't all just happen overnight. There were many meals that were interrupted by various issues, such as, choking, nausea, or emesis. However, by the time he turned one year old, he was pretty much eating on a regular basis but much of the cereal and foods were still not staying down. There was always a constant outfit change going on. Then it dawned on me to try something heavier than the normal cereal and baby food that he had been having such a difficult time with. One day I decided to make a bowl of thick oatmeal. Well of course because of the different texture he was not as receptive of this new meal, but as persistent as he was about not accepting, I was twice as persistent that he would. So after a battle of wills, we had victory!! Oatmeal became our best friend. Then the introduction of the variety boxes came.....yessss, an even bigger hit. This is one of those times that you have to truly learn to be content in whatever state you find yourself in. Who would have ever thought that a bowl of oatmeal could bring my life so much joy? Well it did. Not only was I happy to watch his face light up when it was time to eat, he began to understand that he would be able to enjoy eating. I also was excited that the struggle had diminished in regard to getting something in him that was healthy, had substance and would allow him to be able to continue to grow.

Now, I had two sons who were conquering their challenge of being able to eat and they both were in love with oatmeal. There were times I would go shopping and my cart would have upwards of 10 boxes of oatmeal, a slew of cinnamon applesauce packs or jars (to mix in the oatmeal to make it heavier), many packs of yogurt for snacks and of course lots of Gatorade. That was it. That was all. This is what the ultimate meal would consist of for the both of them for years to come.

At some point, I can't remember when, I decided to sit the both of them together (as if I had a choice) and just make big bowls and feed them both at the same time, alternating almost as an assembly line. They liked it and I loved it. This alleviated the both of them pushing one or the other out of the way rallying for the next spoonful of oatmeal coming their way. At times it was too funny watching them use their strength and thought process in order to out move and outwit the other.

As Rodell grew, his appetite increased to that which put him on "big boy" status. Meaning, the oatmeal was no longer filling him up. At one point he would sit and eat three packs of oatmeal, have a cup of applesauce and then still look for something else to eat. So it was time to move on to bigger and better things. I tried to offer him different tastes and textures in order to see where my next move would be concerning his meals. As I was debating what to add to his diet, one day he simply showed me on his own. While I was eating, he decided to lean in and take a nice big bite of the chicken I was eating all on his own. He looked at me with a greasy mouthful and said "mmmm"!! At that point it was on and popping. For those who have had the pleasure of being around him in the latter years understand what I'm referring to. He was totally in love with chicken. Every time we drove past a fast food chicken restaurant, he would point and say "umma get get"!!! He would repeat it over and over until I either pulled into the parking lot or I drove where it was out of sight leaving him craning his neck watching out the back window with a cry ready to come out of his mouth. I know this sounds sad, but if it were left up to him, we would be stopping by a chicken place or any 7-11 or Circle K (in Charlotte) to fulfill his want, except at these stores it would include pink lemonade and a pack of white powdered doughnuts. So needless to say in order to get from one destination to another in a rush I had to duck and dodge and hit side streets (in both VA and NC) in order not to stop at every single establishment that carried his treats.

As Rodell got older I started to notice that he was still having a hard time swallowing and keeping his foods down. His appetite was great and he would always finish his bowls of oatmeal and his chicken. However, shortly after (and sometimes during) his meals, I could bet money that he would be regurgitating most of his foods. There were even many occasions that his foods (and liquids) would come out of his nose. Now if you remember, I mentioned that Rodney was born with a cleft of the soft palate. I started noticing the same incidences surrounding Rodell's meals so I mentioned it to his pediatrician. I explained that I believed he also had a cleft of the soft palate, however after examination that idea was shot down. I was given the explanation that I needed to cut his foods up even more and then monitor the amounts he was putting in his mouth. So, I left the appointment, still not positive that this information was the full picture of what was going on. However, I'm not a physician so I agreed to follow the advice given and see if a change would occur.

I chopped and monitored and even spoon fed him myself for quite some time afterward and as I expected, there was no change. Naturally, with me being who I have always been, I couldn't just settle with what I believed was a misdiagnosis. So, using my better judgement, I made another call to his pediatrician and requested another appointment. During that appointment, she re-examined his mouth and again said she disagreed and did not see a cleft palate. However, there was something in me and about this situation that pushed me forward to seek a different answer. So, I stressed the symptoms yet again and reminded her of Rodney's journey from birth with his cleft. By the end of that conversation, the pediatrician was so frustrated with me that she looked at me and stated, "Ms. Randolph, it is extremely rare for two siblings to be born with a cleft of the soft palate." I believe at that point I must have looked at her like she was crazy. Yes I knew that piece of data (I had found several articles years ago when Rodney was born). However, I suppose the look that I gave her must have said just what I was thinking.

So with her look of frustration on her face, she asked me what was wrong. I simply looked at her and said, "Yes, I know it's rare, but, we, my boys and I, are also rare. This was God's plan so who are we to say what He should or should not make? So with that being said, I would like a referral to a specialist to examine him please." It was at this point I gained another level of confidence in advocating for my boys. The physician, handed me a referral to see a maxillofacial physician. I thanked her graciously and with a victorious feeling, left her office.

Approximately six weeks later, I took Rodell to his appointment with the specialist. I went in armed with the referral and the documentation from his pediatrician. After the routine question and answer session, the doctor began to examine him. Of course, since this was a new face, Rodell was not going to make it an easy visit. First, he decided he was not going to allow the doctor to get anywhere near him, so he kicked and squirmed and screamed at the doctor. I finally got him to calm down after a long struggle, only for the doctor to say now it was time to examine the inside of his mouth. You got it. A brand new tussle began then. I finally had to strong arm him in one of my many self-taught body holds (no professional training here, it was all about safety and security mommy style). The physician was able to look inside his mouth and just as he was removing his gloved fingers, Rodell bit him. Fortunately, the doctor was not bothered by it and kept on with his assessment. Once I was able to calm Rodell down and picked up the items he had kicked and knocked over during the examination, I gathered our belongings to meet the doctor in his office. I sat there holding my breath, pretty much knowing what he was going to say. He looked up at me and said, "Rodell has what we call a sub-mucous cleft of the soft palate, Ms. Randolph." At that very moment, a rush of relief overcame me. Not the kind of relief you get from being excited because something is complete or finally at an end. It was a relief to know that I had maintained the strength and perseverance to push through and advocate for what I knew was right and needed for my son. I looked at the doctor and merely asked him what needs to be done. He explained to me that while he was forming in the womb, his palate was attempting to form (which explains the thin layer of "mucous-like skin") over top of the cleft portion of his soft palate. In plain and simple words, his palate was closed except for a small pin hole and it needed to be repaired. It would entail in and out surgery and should not present any major problems afterward. So we scheduled his surgery, it ended successfully and opened up the door for him to be able to eat and thoroughly enjoy all foods without any further incidences of choking or regurgitation. I was ever so grateful that I had been given the "I'm no quitter" type of spirit. It has helped me through the years in raising my boys on many occasions.

With the surgery and healing behind us, I decided (or more like he decided) that he wanted to eat any and everything in sight. One of the next things that he decided was going to be a part of his everyday eating habits was peanut butter. We started off with the tip of a spoon of peanut butter and progressed to peanut butter and jelly sandwiches daily. Before long, he was going into the cabinet and finding the peanut butter on his own along with a spoon and bringing it to me. I would try and make a sandwich and most times he would eat it, but eventually he was able to make himself clear because after eating the sandwich he would still reach for the jar. I eventually figured out that it wasn't just the pb&j sandwiches that he wanted (although he dared not turn them down), he wanted to just sit and eat the peanut butter out of the jar. This became a daily ritual. It was such a delight to him that I would have to (much like with chicken places) detour from the peanut butter aisles while in the grocery stores in order not to have to purchase another jar. It wasn't that I did not want to buy him the peanut butter, it was that most days, we already had at least three jars at home. Not only was he a big fan of peanut butter, but he would not accept, pick up or eat anything other than Jif. I would try and purchase other brands that may have been on sale, nope, he wasn't having it. I would try to switch the jars out at the checkout and he would watch the cashier so intently that it eventually became impossible. Most of the cashiers knew him from his peanut butter that they automatically knew by a signal from me to either pretend to ring it up (then hide it from him) or to actually ring it up, and if so, place it in his own bag so he can carry it out of the store. There were times that the ducking and dodging to the peanut butter aisles and moving the jar(s) from one cabinet to another at home to keep him from finding it in hopes that he would eat something else, became a bit tiresome. However, just as most of us forget to remember a blessing, those moments would soon be replaced with the remembrance of when he could not eat at all. So in being a thankful mother, our peanut butter appetizer, meal, dessert and snack carried on as he so desired.

As I stated previously, once the surgery was deemed a success, Rodell showed a love for food that was increasing before my very own eyes. Every time I turned around, he was either leaning over my plate saying "mmmmmm" (his way of saying he wanted some), or he was getting something out of the cabinet or refrigerator and bringing it to me saying "umma...get get" (his way of saying he wanted it or even give it to me). His next level of foods (or should I say his next passion) was frozen dinners. I had picked up a kid's dinner one day just to see if he would eat it....he did. Thereafter, every time we were in the store he had to have those. From those he moved to frozen chicken meals or spaghetti meals. Now don't get things twisted, the child was

52

not surviving off of frozen and/or processed foods, these were his daily snacks after school. The boy had an appetite that was akin to a pre-teen who was going to school, playing sports, and working all day. He could definitely put the food away and I was not going to complain. I loved watching him eat with that goofy grin and hearing that infamous "mmmmm" when he was enjoying it. It was truly a blessing.

WHEN MOTHER IS TIRED

This is a chapter of my life that I initially had decided not to share in my book. However, I cannot speak on my journey with all of its trials, tribulations, and victories and not allow you into the darkest part and giving you a praise report of the outcome. So, again as I take a deep breath I want to share with you one of the most heart wrenching portions of my journey that I have ever had to deal with.[9]

When we become a parent, one of the last things on our mind is being separated from our children. Of course, we know of the temporary separation linked with work, school and their growing personal relationships with their peers along with everything else that life brings us. However, what we are rarely faced with or need to make a decision about, is separating ourselves from them in order to continue to provide their needs, take care of their mental and emotional beings, but most importantly to care for yourself.

This is the state of mind I found myself in as I spoke on earlier. That one day when I found myself so overwhelmed that I had to allow other individuals to do what I was having such a difficult time doing. Now let me start off with saying the mere thought of anyone else other than me being a parental figure over Rodney and Rodell made my skin crawl. Not only as a mother who had dedicated her life to caring for their every need but add in the fact that they were not verbal which terrified me to the core. How could I begin to trust that someone other than myself would be as gentle, yet firm,

---

[9] "We sent him so that none of you would be upset by the troubles we have now. You yourselves know that we must have these troubles." *1Thessalonians 3 (NIV)*

loving but a disciplinarian when needed, to the two boys that were a major part of my life. What if they were not happy? What if they were mistreated, abused, not fed properly, not bathed, or abandoned all together?

In reiterating on the initial phone call to the local mental health agency in Charlotte in order to set up an appointment for Rodney, to get him seen by a neurologist for his medications. I was having a very difficult time during our conversation and had to keep asking her to hold on while I stopped to take care of the boys. So you can only imagine what types of things were going through my mind when I was being asked the question by the mental health social worker inquiring if I wanted her to send help. In my mind the two answers quickly battled one another, of course I did want help versus no I'm good and do not need any help. On my journey, I had prided myself with not having to reach out for help in the day to day care of taking care of the boys. Don't get me wrong, there were a few select individuals who would sit with me, a few who would volunteer so I could run to the store, and a few (very few) who I could count on being in the trenches with me battling it out with the boys. Most times I just didn't want to burden anyone (because at times being the "different ones" many people made me feel as if it was a burden) to ask them to step up and help. Therefore, when posed this question from those in an authority position, I hesitated, thought, then trusted and said yes.

At that very moment upon answering yes, the tears just flowed and flowed because I was in a place where I realized I was tired. Mentally, physically, emotionally drained, bruised all over my body and felt like I couldn't do this another day on my own. It seemed as though just a few mere moments had passed as I had given my answer of yes before there was a knock at my door and the social worker on the phone informs me that on the other side of the door should be my help so I am going to hang up once you have answered the door and allowed them to come into your home.

Once I opened the door, I hung the phone up and allowed the social workers from Child Protective Services (CPS) to come in. I learned that CPS is not just for negative situations regarding parental neglect but can be helpful in many other areas. Along with them were also three police officers from the local police department. They walked in as if they were coming into a hostile environment, cautiously looking around my home. Once they realized they were not in any type of danger, everyone stood/sat in the living room area. I began answering all of the questions that were being asked of me.

Now comes the moment that I will never forget. Rodney gets off the sofa to come stand by me and as he did, Rodell decided he was not going to be left out of the equation. However as he decided to come stand, he noticed that one of the officers was attempting to befriend his brother. Well, let the games begin because even in their own world, it's always competitive and Rodell was not about to let Rodney make a friend and get attention that he wasn't getting. So he did what came natural to him and reached over to scratch his Rodney's face in order to get his brother away from the individuals that were doting over him and giving him compliments.

Well, if you have paid any attention to anything that I have touched on regarding the boys and their behaviors you already know that this was the start of a brand new fight. At the initial scratch, Rodney lunged toward his younger brother and in turn Rodell went for what he knew. They began screaming, scratching at, attempting to bite one another all at the same time running circles around the police officers who had this look like they were in a tornado and couldn't figure out when the eye was going to throw them out and where they would land. As each boy ran past one of the officers, each officer would attempt to grab and stop one or the other, only for each one to wiggle their way loose in a blink of an eye and land another punch or scratch on their brothers' body. This went on for several minutes. I wasn't sure if I was seeing right or not, but it looked to me as if I was watching something from the Keystone Cops and the boys were definitely looking a lot better than the trained officers.

By the time the officers were able to get control of the situation (because the social workers wanted to sit and answer questions and was sure that the officers could handle them lol), all three officers were out of breath. Eventually, one officer decided to speak up and say, "Ma'am I take my hat and badge off to you because you say you have been doing this alone. It's three of us and we can't handle these two strong, rambunctious little boys." At that time I felt like I was in a dream. I heard them, however, it just didn't register quite as quickly as I heard the words. I honestly do not think they were waiting for a response, I believe it was just a statement. They quickly turned their full attention back to the boys as I did the same with the two ladies sitting with me.

I was asked a bunch of questions about who we were, where we came from, family, and friends. I remember them asking and I remember answering most. However, there was a slot of time that I believe I was not fully aware of what exactly was going on. I know now, that it was during this time, (one of my darkest and a rare moment), that God took the wheel of this ride. Even now as I sit back and write all about it, I get a clearer sense that He was in total control of the situation and had His loving arms wrapped all around me.[10]

I remember being asked if they could see the boys' room and I walked them upstairs. It was then, that I started to come back toward my center (as close as I could get). Since the boys were a big part of my life, I was always happy to share about them. So inside of their bedroom I explained my methods of keeping safety and order for not just them but me also. My color coding from hangers to bedroom furnishings for each child would allow not only easy understanding for me but also for any stranger that would walk into their room. Anyone would be able to figure out that Rodney's belongings were red, while Rodell's were blue (their headboards allowed for that determination with a photograph of each child on it).

I then, led them back downstairs to my kitchen area and showed them my routine for feedings and the few medications that each one of them were dispensed daily. It was there, that we decided to sit at the dining table to further discuss my options. As I watched and listened to each person with their encouraging words as well as their empathies of what my duties as a mother were, I knew where the conversation was headed.

The end result was, they wanted to make sure I received some rest. Respite in fact. It was also stated that they

---

[10] If you say, "The Lord is my refuse, and you make the Most High your dwelling, no harm will overtake you, no disaster will come near your tent. For He will command His angels concerning you to guard you in all your ways. They will lift you up in their hands so that you will not strike your foot against a stone." *Psalm 91:9-12 (NIV)*

strongly encourage me to follow up with one of the therapists that they were making a referral to for my sake. Now, those that know me personally, know that I looked at them like they were crazy. I chose my words very carefully and said, "There is nothing wrong with me or my thought process. Why are you referring me to therapy?" One of the social workers just kind of chuckled and reached for my hand and said ever so gently, "Oh Ms. Randolph, we know there is nothing wrong with you. What we do know is that you have been through a great deal in such a short time and you just need to get it out before it does start to have some sort of effect on you. You are emotionally, physically and probably mentally tired. This is not a case of abuse nor neglect. This is one of those situations where we see a parent who has done an excellent job in taking care of her children and she is just a tad bit overwhelmed right now." With that being said, they offered to take the boys. My mind started screaming as I was listening "Take my boys?? What??!!!! Noooo!!! You all have got to be crazy!!!!" Now it was either my mind saying all of this or I said it out loud and wasn't aware that I was being vocal. Both workers looked at me with a combination of fear and sadness across their faces.

I'm sure several minutes passed (at least it felt like it). All I knew was that I was being handed tissue to clean my face and wipe my eyes. This had to be a dream. Or more like a nightmare. There was no way that I was going to allow these women to walk out of this house with my children. My boys. My life. As I began to speak, one of the workers decided to stop me and asked if she could continue on. She stated to me that this would be a voluntary placement and that they would be able to place the boys in the same residence. This, according to them would be an opportunity for me to go to the many places, that I needed to go to in order to get services set up for myself as well as them in Charlotte. They went on to explain to me that I would have a say in every part of their care because they were not being taken away. I would also have access to visit them and bring them home for visits whenever I chose to do so. The only requirement that they would make of me would be that I do follow up and speak with someone to ensure that I was able to release all that I had been holding inside over the years.

After all that was said, I hesitantly agreed to what was placed before me. I had to accept the fact that I was definitely exhausted, mentally, physically and emotionally. I had not had a real break from them since 1997 other than the few hours that they were in school daily.

Once all of the questions were asked regarding their day to day welfare and needs, the workers helped me to pack some of the initial belongings of the boys. It was a moment in time that I would never forget. The feelings that started to consume me of guilt, shame and almost defeat. As a human but more so as a mother. There were many moments during this time as we gathered clothing, pull-ups and medications that I opened my mouth to stop the whole process. However, there was one worker that was more in tuned to what I was going through emotionally, and she just kept coming over to me and giving me a side hug or rubbing my back saying things like, "it's ok", or "it will be alright", or "you've got the strength needed to do this" and lastly, "God's got you Ms. Randolph." I couldn't respond. I felt as if I were walking around having an out of body experience. I was in I guess what they call a twilight zone.

After we carried the necessary belongings downstairs and set them by the front door. One of the workers at that point said she needed me to sign some consent papers that she would go over with me. This process took a bit longer than anticipated because I would become a little antsy prior to every initial and signature.

Finally, they said they needed to load the suitcases into the car. The workers asked the officers if they would do so while I took a few minutes with the boys. It was then, I realized I needed to ensure that wherever the boys ended up, there would need to be some written instruction about their daily care. I asked one of the workers if I could take a few minutes to do just that before they left. She agreed. So I took the time to write up their daily routine, from sunrise to breakfast and what and how they would eat it; their snacks, other meals, bath times, outdoor times and finally bedtime. I also included some of their aggressive behavior triggers and mentioned that when one was having a meltdown the other was sure to feed off his anger and join in. I also included who was to wear what (in order to distinguish whose clothes belonged to who) because I wanted to ensure that they were still being well kept in my absence (something that I have always been extremely detailed about because they were always on the receiving end of long stares because of their disability, so I wanted to make sure that if they were stared at, that they look as decent and clean as possible). Once my notes were completed, I handed it to the worker and said "ok, I'm ready."

I walked over to my sons and my heart felt as if it were swelling up in my chest. I thought it was going to burst. All types of thoughts started flowing through my mind and tears started streaming down my face. I felt as if I was failing my sons. I held on to each one as best as I could (because with the strangers in the house they just weren't giving any type of cooperation). I explained to them they were going for a ride in the car and were going to sleep somewhere else and that I would see them very soon. To this day, I'm still sure that they were not clear on everything that I said to them. However, if nothing else, when I said "I love you guys", they gave me the biggest hugs I had every received from them.

Of course, the hugs at the end of my talk did not help at all because immediately following, the workers started to take the boys outside to the cars and that bought on more emotions for me. The workers asked me to stay inside the house while they and the officers placed the boys in the car. Rodney and Rodell went relatively peaceful (because riding around in the car was our calming trick on most days anyway). As I stood in the doorway watching them being placed in their seats in the back of the car, I had to fight back the urge to scream. A scream that I could feel bubbling from my gut. I knew that if I let it out it would start a domino effect with the boys and that definitely was not needed at this point. Once inside the car, the workers spoke to one another and one got in the driver's side and the other came back to me and said "Ms. Randolph, we truly admire your strength and want to tell you that you are a woman of great courage. We will be praying for and with you. God bless."

She then turned around to get into her vehicle. As she started to put her car in gear, I could hear the familiar screams of the boys. They were not screams of terror or crying out for me. They were the screams from fighting. They were going at it in the back of the CPS car. The other worker looked terrified and jumped out of the car and opened the back door. As I ran out toward the car, she held her hand up and requested I stay back and allow them to figure it out. Well I must say they figured it out and ended up placing Rodney in the vehicle with the second social worker. The boys were used to having their own space and they achieved it. Once they were separated, all was calm and they were able to leave.

Imagine being in a strange place and having someone walk up to you and say to your child "come here and leave with me" and they take their hand and walk away with them. That pain, despair and confused state is one that I would not wish on another mother or anyone else in this world…ever!

I walked into my house and shut my door and slid down the door until I hit the floor. Feelings started to pour out. My emotions were all awry. I felt as if my whole world had just come to a screeching halt. Someone hit the brakes on my vehicle really hard yet at the same time I was hit from behind by a vehicle driving 85 mph. The feeling of being thrown from the car and you know you are falling but not sure when you will hit the ground and when you do, what type of shape you will be in. Then here comes the gutter cries. The one that starts as a deep moan and comes bubbling up into your throat that before you can get it out you are already choking and coughing and feeling ill and tears are falling and your head is banging like someone hitting it with a sledge hammer.

My cries eventually lead to a plea. I begin to plead to God and ask him why this was happening. What did I do so wrong to end up here was my next question to Him. I sat there, not sure for how long, but I know it was a good while. I managed to get myself to my feet and went to the sofa and just curled up, cried and rocked myself to sleep.

At some point, my telephone starts to ring with family members calling to check on me and my emotional status. It was at that point, that I began to receive what they only knew how to give and that was the encouraging words of "you need this time to rest", "take your time and get some sleep" and God only knows what else was said because I honestly don't remember.

At some point during the night, I made my way upstairs to try and get some rest. I didn't expect to get much but figured I would at least try. I was correct, sleep definitely didn't come. I laid there with the lights out and just let my mind wander. I worried about whether the boys were safe, afraid, or wondering if I had deserted them. I prayed and asked God to forgive me for not having the strength to push through what He had given me as my assignment. I asked Him to dispatch His angels around my boys to keep them safe from all dangers. I asked if He would keep any sexual predators away. That was always one of my biggest concerns for them since they were not verbal and would not be able to tell anyone if they in fact had been subject to abused of any type. I prayed that God would also open whatever doors that He wanted me to go through in order to get to the place where He wanted me to be. I asked that He open the doors and place the right persons in front of me to be able to get the necessary services started for the boys. Lastly, I thanked Him for the clarity that I needed and that only He could give me concerning this whole situation.

On any given night, after I have said my prayers, I would easily drift off to sleep. Not that night. My mind was still racing. So I got up and slowly walked through each room and just stood for a while, taking in the silence and again saying a quick silent prayer. As I found myself downstairs in the kitchen, I made some coffee because I figured I was going to have a sleepless night. Once armed with my cup of coffee I proceeded to my computer and researched the services available within the City.

A NEW BEGINNING

Dawn. It was there before I knew it. No sleep whatsoever and running off pure adrenaline. I prepared myself to go out and get the ball rolling for our needs in this new place. By mid-morning (it was a Saturday) the only thing I could do was drive around and see where these unknown roads would lead me to. I located nearby schools, grocery stores, social services and malls. Mental notes were made as to what and where I would return to on Monday.

It was later that day, I received a phone call from my mom indicating that one of my favorite gospel artists had a church in Charlotte. A fact that I was not aware of. In hindsight, I now understand why I was led to this area. I researched and found the address for the church and made a conscious decision to go there the next day for morning services. By late evening, sleep deprivation started to get the best of me, so I tried my hand yet again. In the middle of my bed, I found myself in a fetal position (those who have ever experienced deep hurt can relate to this). As the emotions started to kick in again, I allowed myself to feel what I had been attempting to block out for the majority of the day. Pain. Despair. In that position, I wept until I fell asleep. I woke some hours later in the middle of the night startled and jumped up wondering where my boys were. Once my thoughts came back to me, a feeling of emptiness started to take over me. It was at this time, I decided to not focus as much (if at all possible) on what had just happened over the last couple of days, but to think about what was and needed to happen from that point on.

I decided to go through with my plans to attend church services, so I prepared myself for that. It was so very different having the extra time preparing myself for anything. I was so used to having a detailed plan of preparing for an outing. Even though Rodney and Rodell were ages eight and five at the time, it was as if I had two toddlers to plan and prepare for. In addition, to preparation, the time it took to bathe, feed and dress them was now a large open slot in my day.

By the time I arrived at the church, my emotions were all over the place. I walked into the church and immediately felt a strange feeling as if every emotion had been forced out of me. I don't know if it were a sense of comfort or what. I just know that I felt a kinship to being in a loved one's arms that allowed you to just let it all out. So as I tried to walk toward the sanctuary, I was met by a gentle woman who evidently saw my distress. She immediately walked up to me and wrapped her arms around me and shuffled me to the ladies room. It was here that (unbeknownst to me at the time), a friendship with an angel was started. Her love for God showed so brightly during our first encounter that upon her inquiring "sister is there something I can help you with? You are in the right place. God is in the midst of us here."

Once we went through our introductions, I proceeded to tell her what I had been through over the last 72 hours. She looked at me and leaned in and held me so tight and began to pray. During this prayer, there were a few key words that stuck with me through the years. The words that we use day to day in our prayers and communication, meant so much to me on this day. She prayed for my healing, comfort, and peace beyond all understanding. It was one of the most powerful moments I had encountered in my entire life.

She then led me into the church and I realized I was at a no turning back point in my life. I began worshipping weekly, then adding in a weekly bible study and eventually started singing in the choirs. I could feel myself learning, leaning more on Jesus and allowing myself to forgive me with the complete understanding that all of what I had been through was all part of God's plan for me.

There are times in life that we must go through some of the toughest trials in order for God to get our attention totally. I had a relationship with Christ. At least I believed I did. I had at that time in my life the kind of relationship with Him that consisted of me calling on Him only when I needed Him (like most of us have a tendency to do). In hindsight, I know that what He wanted from (and for) me, was to have a daily walk with Him. To acknowledge His presence in everything that I go through and do. To learn what His promises were and stand on them before, during and after my storms. To bless Him and honor Him each and every day and to know that no matter what I endured, that all was well. [11]

Once I got a true understanding of all that was expected of me, it was then that my head and the fog that I was in started to clear up.

I eventually made the call and appointment to speak to a therapist. I am usually not nervous but for this occasion, I found my palms to be real sweaty. During my first session, there was the usual question and answer game. At the end of that session, the counselor says, you have just been keeping everything all bottled up. You have to find an outlet

---

[11]"But whoever listens to me will live in safety and be at ease, without fear or harm." *Proverbs 1:33 (NIV)*

so it doesn't continue to clutter up your mind. She told me I needed to find me some quality time for myself and learn to pamper me and relax. Well that was easier said than done on most days. However, I told her I would make every effort to do so. She also requested that I jot down in an outline some of my most important life events and bring it back to my next session with her. Of course, being in the mental health realm of things, she wanted to prescribe me some medications to help me to sleep. I told her that I would try them but could not guarantee that I would stick to it because I was so accustomed to being alert even in my sleep.

So I left my appointment feeling calmer than when I arrived. As I arrived home, I received a phone call from the social worker. I had intended on calling her once I got home anyway to see how the boys were settling in. She begins to explain to me that they were going to have to separate the boys immediately. She said the woman that they were with called and said she couldn't do the both of them and that they were entirely too much for one person. According to the report she received, the boys were constantly fighting, screaming at one another, and with all of their other issues, it was just too much for the woman. She also said the woman stated that it was no wonder the mom had a breakdown and she was surprised that it had not happened earlier than this. So the worker stated they needed to meet with me so we could discuss things a little more in depth. We set up a time to meet later that day.

RODNEY'S NEW PLACE

Later that day at the meeting, the team of workers assured me that they wanted me to be comfortable with whatever decision we came up with. So several options were placed on the table, one being the boys go to separate homes and the other was Rodell go to another home and Rodney be placed in a facility where he could receive 24 hour care (which he needed because he was more medically fragile). As I asked questions pertaining to future visitations, et al, the team of workers ensured that as time went on they would keep me updated on everything as well as including me in all of their care.

Since I had decided to place Rodney in the facility, we set up an appointment so I could tour the place and meet some of the staff. Upon arrival, I must say I was taken aback. The first reason was because the facility was in such a secluded area (which later it was revealed it was for the residents' safety). Secondly, once inside and during the tour, the various wings reminded me of an older hospital or actually what it really was.....a facility. Needless to say I was not too pleased, however, I knew that in order for me to get back on track I needed to ensure that Rodney was in a safe environment where he could receive all of the care he required. By the end of the meeting, I had agreed with the placement (now we just had to wait for the availability of space).

Once an available bed was ready for Rodney's admission, I drove to the facility to get him acclimated. Of course, I had to brighten up his room and put some color in it. I had painstakingly taking the time to ensure that his name was on the inside of every piece of clothing item (shoes included).

I sat with my son for a while and prayed over him and assured him that I would be back. It was heart wrenching, but I had to hold my head up and my tears back so he would not be able to sense my emotions.

Over time (months), I was back and forth visiting as well as bringing him home for visits, some over nights and some weekends as well as holidays. We settled into our routine of back and forth. There were several individuals whom I had the pleasure of bonding with at the facility and they became Rodney's extended family. They were my eyes and ears of everything concerning Rodney. I was able to sleep knowing that God had yet again placed angels around us.

Of course, during the time that Rodney was a resident of the facility I found myself still beating myself up and very emotional. There was always a big void in every part of each day that passed.

As a mother, I ensured that I was available to make it to every event and/or function. I just did not want to be "that mom" out of the large number of residents, who was never there. On top of that, I always wanted to make sure that Rodney did not feel as if I had deserted him.

There was one time in particular, it was right before Christmas and there was a holiday luncheon set up for the residents and their families. Of course, the enemy is known for showing his ugly head (because he comes to take us out and away from our purpose)[12], I ran into all types of

---

[12] "The thief comes only to steal and kill and destroy; I have come that they may have life, and have it to the full." *John 10:10 (NIV)*

problems early that morning. As I went downstairs to make my coffee I found the coffee had perked, but I had not placed the pot all of the way on the burner so as the coffee was dripping it was running on the side of the pot all on the kitchen floor (Obstacle #1). Once I got all of it cleaned and made a second pot and was able to get some into my system, I remembered, telling myself that everything would be fine at that point.

Who was I kidding? I start to prepare myself to get dressed and as I walk from the closet to my bed, I stump my toe on the bed and lose my balance and of course, I fall and knock my coffee over on the floor. (Obstacle #2). Uugghh!!!! You can imagine I wanted to take my cup and just throw it at this point. Moving as quickly as I could, I cleaned that mess up also.

Alright, here I go, time to get dressed. I put on my jeans, throw on my shoes, sweater and grab a belt. Then realized I had not fastened up my jeans. Easy right? Nope. As I fasten them, the zipper comes totally off track and the pulley breaks off!! (Obstacle #3). Are you kidding me? Easy enough fix. So I just grab another pair of jeans and then I'm good to go.

I gather everything to that I will need to take with me to the luncheon and set it by the door. I proceed outside to my car and put everything inside and settle myself down in the seat relieved that I'm finally leaving. Or am I? I go to start my car and yes......nothing. No sound. It won't turn over. Absolutely nothing. (Obstacle #4). Oh you can only imagine some of the choice words that were coming out of my mouth at that time (don't judge me; I haven't always been saved and attempting to live right). I make a few phone calls to see who is around and can help me. No one is available. My mind is racing as I look at the time and realize that in a few minutes I will be late. My heart is pounding, all types of thoughts are going through my head. Then all of a sudden something tells me to get back in the car and try it again. Bingo!!! I've got live action this time. By this time, I'm smiling and then I'm on my way. With my adrenalin still pumping because I have a good 25 minute drive to get to my son, I maneuver through traffic and actually make it there in one piece. As I'm rushing through the doors to get to Rodney, I run inside the party area with tears in my eyes (because I didn't want him to think that I had forgotten about him and just not showed up). However, as I look around for him he is just about the only one around. I apologetically hug him and explain to the staff why I'm so late and begin to apologize for my lateness. The staff tells me it's not necessary and that she understands and that actually, I'm pretty much the only parent there. Hold on. What? Did I hear her correct? I asked her what she had said and can she please repeat that. She did so and I must have been there with my mouth hanging wide open because as she looked at me she slowly nodded her head as if to say "you heard me right".

It was at that moment I was heartbroken. Not for me or Rodney any longer, but for the other residents who I realized didn't have the luxury of a parent having to face all types of mishaps just to get to them and push through it. Even though I had been beating myself up still about his placement at the facility, at that particular moment, I realized that nothing on this earth could separate me from him. We were truly blessed. Tears fell at that point. Not tears of sadness. Have you ever felt so much love for someone that you just shed a tear for them at that particular moment? He hugged my neck and gave me a sloppy kiss on the cheek and made his funny grunting noise in my ear and I knew that all was well with him. I made a mental note to myself that I needed to work on putting together a plan to bring my son home. As soon as I possibly could.

The holiday season was great. I bought both boys home and we had a good time (still fighting) and everything else. It was just like old times. The one thing that was different was I found myself with just a little bit more patience and strength. What a difference a half a year made in our lives.

During this holiday break I decided I would take them to church. We arrived and what came next was something I had not planned or even expected. As we were going across the parking lot, Rodell decided he didn't want to go into this strange place. He could hear music coming from inside the building and it would catch his attention for a brief second or two, however, he would quickly forget about it.

It was during those times that he had forgotten about the music that became difficult. Not being a person that easily transitioned, the fight began. He started with his brother and as I leaned in attempting to walk at the same time, he swung on me. Woooosaahhhh!! Do you remember those times when your mother would grab you by your arm or hand and talk between her clenched teeth explaining to you that you better not show off and come on before she gives you something to cry about? Well I had one of those mother moments. Flanked by a son on both sides, I walked as upright as I could into the church. I was determined not to have the enemy steal our joy. Once the boys realized I had gotten them into the church, one started pulling away from me in one direction and of course the other went the opposite way. Rodney was relatively easy to redirect toward the direction we needed to go. It was the other one, Rodell, the leader, the one with that attitude of 'you can't tell me what to do or where to go'. He started kicking and screaming and attempting to fall on the floor as I pulled and shoved them at the same time toward a seat. Some people looked, others attempted to walk toward us as if to help then stopped, eventually we were spotted by the young woman who came to my aid on my first visit to the church. She helped me to maneuver the boys down to the front of the church and we got them settled and that was that. We had church.

By the time, service was over and we returned to the house, both boys were tired, hungry and ready for a nap. Yes at five and eight years of age they were still taking naps. It was my refuge time. I needed to be able to regroup in order to make it through the remainder of the day and prepare myself for the mental and emotional feelings I would have to face the next day returning them.

The days, weeks and months began to slip by and I was truly beyond a doubt much stronger and felt refreshed. There were less frustrating moments to deal with and I was beginning to be hopeful. Although there were times when going to visit, sit with or even take Rodney home with me, I would become a bit perturbed. No, it wasn't because of Rodney. It was because of individuals that just didn't treat him as I would. Don't get me wrong as I stated earlier, he had some wonderful angels around him. They were the best! However, as we all know wherever there is good, evil lurks around the corner. Now when I speak of evil, I mean just the kind of selfish attitude(s) that think only about themselves. I say this because, there were at least a handful of times that I would come to pick him up to visit and some of his personal items could not be located. It didn't particularly matter what it was, there was always something missing. From his sneakers, to clothes to blankets. You name it. Now for those that know Miss Trenny (she is my unsaved alter ego), she had to pay a few visits to the facility in hopes that she would catch someone slipping and make them pay for the disappearance of Rodney's property. So on one of these visits Miss Trenny decided that it would behoove everyone involved (and then some) to search for and locate these missing items. Let's just say, most of them were found before I departed from that visit. There were items that still were not located and Miss Trenny ensured that the staff was aware of where to go to purchase, replace them and what size(s) and/or colors to repurchase them in. Case closed.

Now without going into too much detail, it was just a few months past Rodney's one year that he had been at the facility. I arrived (as usual) to pick him up for a holiday visit. Since it was the holiday, there were a few faces that I was not familiar with working so I was made to follow the normal protocol of waiting for someone to escort me to him (as opposed to my being able to just walk through the facility on my own). After I was escorted to his room to gather whatever items I needed to take with me, I went to the area where I could speak with a staff member and pick up his medications that needed to be given to him while he was with me. I look toward where Rodney is standing and waiting patiently and notice that a staff member is preparing some medications. My motherly instinct kicked in and I slowly eased my way toward the medication area, while making small talk, and began to ask questions about the medications being prepared. While conversing with them, I notice a different type of medication that was unfamiliar to me. I asked the three W's (who, what and why) of this medication. Who prescribed it? What is it for? Why the change? I was then informed that the doctor decided to change it. As you can imagine, I stood there for a brief second and thought that doesn't sound right because I am always kept abreast of any type of changes to his medications as well as diet. So I stop the staff member and tell them that Rodney does not take that medication and he definitely does not take it in that form. However, the staff member insisted that as of now he does and that the physician wrote for the change. The staff member proceeded to walk toward Rodney with his medications (including the new one) as I interject again explain nicely but much firmer that he doesn't take that type of medication. In hindsight, I wish someone from the staff had briefed this new staff member on Miss Trenny and the protocol in which to handle controversial conversations with her. However, they had not warned (or informed) the staff member. As the medication gets closer to Rodney and the staff member attempts to put the medication into his mouth, I lunge at the same time that Rodney is spitting it back out of his mouth. What the staff member did not realize is while they were preparing the medications, I was using my cell phone to look up this new medication and found it to not be a medication that Rodney should be taking. So I lunged toward the staff member and snatch the notebook out of their hand that was holding all pertinent medical information and asked them to show me where this new medication was listed on Rodney's profile. Needless to say, they were not able to do so. Why? Well simply because it was for his roommate and not for Rodney himself. Needless to say, I lost it and the staff member raised their voice at me accusing me of being overly sensitive. Overly sensitive? You are about to dispense a medication to my child which would have a strong possibility of lowering his blood pressure without any hesitation and I'm being overly sensitive. The next thing I remember is several familiar voices asking me to calm down and attempting to keep me from running after this person who had ran down the hall screaming as if they were a woman. I was able to slide my arms out of my jacket and run toward them, however, I did not have any luck finding them.

By the time things had calmed down, I was able to regroup and explain to other staff members of the incident that had just occurred. I checked on my son, packed up his medications, grabbed his bags and explained that I would be writing a letter or two and wanted that person dismissed. By the end of the weekend, my letter was written and sent out along with a request for his removal from the facility along with every personal care and respite service that I was receiving with Rodell without having to be placed on a waiting list. Of course, after several meetings over the next few weeks, I took Rodney out of the facility permanently along with all of the services requested that would be beneficial to the both of us, to include some of the staff that worked at the facility. There were some that I just could not do without and vice versa.

So there was a staff member who was Rodney's second mom. To let her tell it she was his first, she just let me give birth to him for her. She totally adored him and it was likewise for him. She became his community worker. Not just in the community. I should be more accurate and say wherever she went, Rodney went. He would be found riding in the back seat of her car stretched out as if he were being chauffeured around. Or at times he would be in the front seat, riding shot gun alongside her. It was a beautiful relationship. When she smiled, he smiled. When he cried, she cried. Whatever changes I needed to adapt to concerning his needs and any challenges within the community, she was there to assist me (us) through it. If there was something that she knew about and felt it would be beneficial for Rodney, she would bring me the information in as much detail as possible to take to his case management team to request it. This was the beginning of a new way of breathing for me.

The daily hours that she would provide in her home and the community enabled me to become adjust to a new way of caring for both boys. With a few personal care attendants blended with our family, it was as if I had received an opportunity to live again. Rodney so enjoyed the special time that he was able to go out and about in the community. Most days when he was dropped off by the school bus, he refused to come into the house. Since he learned from repetition, he knew that after school one of his care attendants would be picking him up to take him away for a ride, shopping, to the park or just to visit with their family members. I would take him in the house in order to prepare him for his departure, only to find him attempting to sneak out the door in anticipation of whomever was scheduled to pick him up that day.

In an attempt to make our life a little easier, I also chose a husband and wife team to provide respite services for both boys. This choice was made to not only make things easier for me in having to deal with multiple individuals, but it also aided in the transition challenges I knew were to come from Rodell. Respite services were put into place that allowed the boys to leave just about every weekend. This was another positive that came out of my ability to allow God to work things for our good during the storm. Most individuals, are placed on waiting lists for years. However, with my previous involvement with community based agencies, and my ability to advocate, we were blessed to not have the hardship of waiting.

Between myself and the personal care attendants for both boys we were able to add to each other's lives. I honestly don't know how I ever made it without these special angels who loved, nurtured and included Rodney and Rodell in their family compositions. I can only say that it was by the hand of God and His grace and mercy that we were a perfect fit for one another.   I will forever bless Him for these individuals and what He allowed them to bring to our day to lives.

RODELL'S NEW PLACE

Since a decision had been made to separate the boys, Rodell was taken to another home. Long story short, he was placed with a wonderful family. They took him in and treated him as if he was their own flesh and blood. I would visit with him there and they would bring him to my home to visit. We also started rotating weekend visitation into our schedules. In the midst of all of the visits, I too, was ushered into their family. They began to include me in family trips, cook outs, dinners, you name it. They were my family away from my family. After several months of him living with them, I decided that it was time to bring him back home with me.

I contacted the proper individuals and explained that I had been resting, regrouping and I wanted to bring my son back home. There were a few individuals that voiced their opinion otherwise. However, I felt like that break was more than enough and I needed to continue on being a full time mother to my boys, just as God had planned it.

So as plans were being made to bring Rodell back home, I was introduced to some new services. These services would be the next best thing to sliced bread for me. It was Personal Attendant and Respite Care services. Once those services were initiated, of course I chose several of the individuals who had been dealing with him during his time away from me. I wanted to include them, because in my world trust was everything. I needed to be able to continue to trust who I had caring for him. On top of that, I wanted him to continue to be loved by them. He had become such an intricate part of their family and I did not want to take that away from him or them.

During his stay with his new found family (okay I'm going to say it for what it really was since this is all about my therapy – his foster family), the boys were enrolled in a day support program. Well of course, they were assigned to different individuals in different rooms. However, picture them at that stage allowing anyone to tell them "no you can't be in here with your brother" or even "no Rodell, I'm not your worker, I'm Rodney's worker". Needless to say, this particular worker (who ended up being my surrogate little sister even to this day), was forced by Rodell to be his worker. He wasn't taking no for an answer and that was that.

In going to the day support program after school each day, as well as all day during the summer, the boys got into a routine. With Rodell, his routine consisted of ensuring that his choice of who his worker was to be, was kept as he wanted. So each day his worker would pull up to the building and attempt to walk in through a different door. She chose this way because not only would it allow her to get into the building and get settled but also if she was needed to work in a different room, she could do so. Well, that's what she thought anyway. Again, (if you hadn't figured out who was the more aggressive in everything by now), Rodell, had figured out his way around the building and once he saw her car pull up, if she didn't come into the door by his class room, he would run through the building looking in all of the rooms until he found her. I do believe he was in love with her. He didn't want anyone else around her, with her or near her. What does that sound like to you? My boy had a crush on a grown woman. It was too adorable how his entire face would just light up in her presence. She was slowly becoming his world. So, I did what any other mother would do in my situation. I asked her to become his personal care attendant. She agreed.

If you have never believed in a perfect match, I'm here to tell you that it does exist. Rodell's personal care worker was the best. She too, treasured and enjoyed her assignment of being able to work with him. Most days Rodell would come home from school. After he would make his rounds through the house checking all of the rooms (I believed he was always looking to see if anyone was in the house), he would end up in the kitchen for his afternoon snack. Being excited about being home, eating and waiting for his care attendant, he would bounce from the kitchen to the front door. Once he noticed the familiar car pull up in front of the house, he would let a loud yet giggly scream while bouncing on his toes. He was filled with joy daily to see his personal care attendant because he too, knew that it meant, he was in for his daily treat. His day would be made complete, just by the fact that he knew he was going out for a ride. It bought me such joy to see the connection he had with his personal care attendant.

Rodell became so attached to his care attendant that on any given day, he would refuse to get out of the car when he returned home. He wanted to ride. He wanted to listen to the music. He wanted to be a big boy and just hang out with "his girl".

Eventually, Rodell's outings would lead to extended visits. He would travel with his care attendant to South Carolina to visit her family. He would go to basketball games where he would without a doubt have to be restrained from running onto the basketball court in his excitement. Being ushered into this family he also traveled for his attendant families' birthday parties and other functions. He was blossoming and allowing her to teach him other life skills. His social skills started to improve. Their connection allowed me to open up and include his personal care attendant as a permanent member of my family. This was a win-win situation for all parties involved.

AGGRESSIVE BEHAVIORS

One of the things that was made evident early in Roc's school years was that he did not like change. His ability to transition from one event to another was generally not a smooth one. I remember during his third grade year, he was attending a school in Virginia and at some point during his daily regimen had to change classes for his various therapy sessions (speech/language and occupational). During this time I was also dropping him off and picking him up from school because of his behaviors. It was during this time that every single day that I would come into the school to pick him up one of a few scenarios I would be faced with. It appeared that he was very familiar with his teacher and loved being in her classroom but did not like the fact that he was taken out of class to be with one of the therapists. His inability to grasp that he was to return to the teacher and his familiar surroundings created a hostile child. So on most days I would arrive at the school only to find his teacher going to the nurse holding a part of her body or coming from the clinic with some sort of ice pack on her because she had bumps, bruises, aches and/or pains caused by Rodell. She was a very loving and dedicated teacher and no matter how much he hit at, punched or bit her, she continued to press on determined to provide him with the most conducive educational environment possible.

I can remember the first time I arrived at the school to pick him up and he was not in his classroom. His teacher quickly escorted me to where he was in another room. She explained to me that he had been having issues with his aggressiveness and they found it necessary to separate him from the rest of the class for everyone's safety as well as a way to provide him with a cool down atmosphere. Of course, in dealing with him, I already knew that being separated from the classroom and his peers wasn't going to do him any justice. (No one wants to feel isolated when going through a situation such as this and made to feel they are "the problem"). However, as a realistic parent I understood the reasoning for the separation. As I walked closer to the classroom, I could hear my son's screams. Again, these screams were not just the screams of someone being injured or crying really loud. You could hear the anger and despair with every outburst. I knew before walking through the closed door that Rodell was angry, his feelings were hurt and he was just not happy. I peeped through the little window only to find him in the room with an assistant. He was walking around a few desks that were out of place (I could easily assume he had pushed them around during his meltdown). As he sensed my presence, he looked up at me through the window with tears streaming down his face and said "umma.....umma" all the while making his kisses sound toward me. The teacher unlocked the door and I walked in totally heartbroken at the scene. After his hugs and kisses to me I walked him back to his class to get his belongings.

There were quite a few more incidences such as this one with some ending in his assigned class while most ending up in the designated "quiet room". It was during this time, that his teacher decided to approach me with the request for an IEP meeting and the suggestions of a different school placement because his current school was not able to handle his behaviors and provide him with the level of behavior therapy he required.

In continuing to be the realistic parent that I had always strived to be with both boys, I agreed to the meeting. It was quickly scheduled and held and within a matter of a couple of weeks, Roc was transferred to a more specialized school that was a better fit for him and his needs. Going to a new school with new faces and schedules was going to be a challenge in itself, however, his big brother Rodney was already a student at the school so I was hoping that this would soften the blow of the transition.

Once he began his new school, it was just as I had expected. He was elated to be getting on the same school bus with his brother. The catch was getting him to not want to go to class with him. That was a feat in itself for the staff. However they assured me that he would be alright and they could handle him. I took their word for it. Initially, they had a few struggles but eventually you could see the change in him. He was in his element and within a classroom setting where he wasn't the only one with challenges.

The only difference in this particular school and his classroom assignment was that Rodell was the smallest one and if memory serves me correct he was one of the youngest students of a class of about five other boys and one female. Being the smallest in the class did not deter his aggressions though. He had quite a few days during one of his meltdowns and aggressiveness he would have some of the older and bigger students (at least 2-4 years his senior and a good 100 lbs more) cringing in the corner. It was at that point in his life that I knew I definitely had a long road still ahead with his behaviors, even with all of the progress we had made to that point. I continued to keep the faith and trust in God, that in due season, his aggressiveness would no longer rule him or his life.

A level of maturity was beginning to show in Rodell's life. He began to follow more directions as they were given from going to pick out the clothes he wanted to wear (there was always the infamous long sleeve blue thermal, a pair of jeans and water shoes) that he felt the need to wear every single day. It was at the point I had to hide these items once he was up in the morning and in the shower. Oh but the fun we had once he was ready to get dressed for school and he was not able to find this beloved outfit of his to wear on that day. I had to get creative with the hiding places because he would often find it and want to put in on to go to school. Hiding places such as under the mattress, in a kitchen cabinet or even behind the towels in the linen closet were ideal on most days. Then there were the days when he would search every single inch of the house up until the very moment the bus would come to pick them up. Some of the other abilities that showed his maturity level and increased cognitive level surrounded being able to go into the kitchen on his own and get what he wanted to eat out of the cabinets from his pb&j, oatmeal, frozen spaghetti dinners (two at a time) to eat. Then there was his ability to realize that he no longer wanted to be wet in his pull-ups. This was something that had been worked on for a number of years. The day that I walked into the bathroom and found an open bag of pull-ups on the floor with a wet one inside the bag, I realized it was definitely time to complete the task. As I cleaned the up after him I also found that he had taken the time to not only peepee in the toilet but there was tissue in the commode also!! Yessss!!! He is a big boy now. He had just shown me without being verbal that he understood what I had been attempting to show and explain to him for years. At the ripe age of eleven years old, my baby boy was a step closer to being a big boy. The most exciting part of this was as I completed my clean up, I went to check on him to see what he had on. lo and behold, he had a pull-up on (backwards) but it was on. As you can only imagine at that time there was nothing but tears, shouts of joy and lots of praise on a job well done, along with lots of kisses to him. This celebration of course led to snacks he wanted. These were just a few of his major accomplishments that were starting to appear in the forefront of his life. This was request number three (for the boys to be potty trained) that had been in my prayers from the beginning.

RODELL PREPARES TO GO HOME

During the summer of 2012 there was a sudden influx of aggressions and head banging going on with Rodell. Most of the incidences were happening at home between the two of us so I figured he was just going through a rebellious state that would lead us to a pre-teen/parent battle. He was determined get his way in any and every situation and most times, I was his obstacle. I had to be alert and on point when I had to deny a request from him, knowing that my denial would surely spark a negative response from him.

Then there were times that out of the blue and no known apparent reason, a meltdown would start just because he was feeling some kind of way. As most knew him, he was an avid music lover and never went anywhere without some sort of music device. One day, he was sitting on the floor, trying to put his water shoes on and listening to the music from his radio and the station gave way to static. He called me to inform me that his music was not playing and said to me "umma get-get". So naturally, I fixed the station. A few minutes later the same thing happened and naturally, I fixed it. Unfortunately, this fix still didn't work long. I believe it was due to the fact that his radio had been dropped many times and it was more than likely on its last leg. This really upset him and instead of allowing me to try and fix it for him, he started full blown tantrum to include banging his head on the floor. As I grabbed him to stop him from hurting himself, he bit me as hard as he could. This episode of course went on for several moments until I was able to get him calm, medicated and in the bed. With the head banging, I was a little concerned about how much damage he could possibly due to himself. So I contacted his psychiatrist to inform him of my concerns and requested to see him immediately. Once we were in our appointment the next day, I really didn't have to say much because the head banging and screaming began in the waiting area of the office so staff was able to witness his behaviors.

During this appointment his psychiatrist and I discussed all of his medications versus his natural psych issues coupled with his aggressive behaviors. He wanted to take him off of his medications he had been on for years and start him on a more "adult like" regimen of medications. However, the only way to do this was to admit him into a psych hospital for children. What??? Are you serious??? This was my reaction. Okay, hold on. I knew a long time ago that I was dealing with the medical issues and a genetic syndrome that my boys had been diagnosed with. Then there was the psych issue they were diagnosed with and that was a double whammy. However, I never in my life had expected to have either one of them placed or committed to a mental health facility. The psychiatrist reassured me that Rodell would be monitored 24 hours a day and that there was a well trained staff there to aid him through the entire process. After discussing it for a while with him I said no. No thank you. Nope. It's ok. So, he just said he understood and if there was no change, or if I ran into an uncontrollable psych issue with him, or if I changed my mind, to just give the office a call and we could move forward from that point. So there were minimal psychotropic medication changes and we went back home to deal with this new level of meltdowns and aggressions.

With the slight change in medications made, it appeared over the new few weeks that Rodell's behaviors were being controlled. The reality of it was not that they were really being controlled but more so he was in the window of adaptation. Any new psychotropic medication leaves you groggy and you are at times a little more subdued. It was evident after the first few weeks, I was having a difficult time getting him ready for bed. He was just not being cooperative at all. I tried everything from being stern, waiting a few minutes, being stern again, bribing him, to making it all into a game for him. All to no avail. Every time I attempted to get him to get ready for bed, his infamous scream where he would look me directly in the eyes and let loose would just bellow out of his body. The evening's events quickly escalated before I knew it. As quickly as the fighting began I looked at my child and saw someone with prodigious strength coming at me. I knew this was going to be a tough one. I tried to calm him down by talking, holding and restraining. Once I was able to get him to the floor he started banging his head. After tussling with him and trying to get him to stop, I reached for my phone and called his psychiatrist. He suggested that I take him somewhere that he could get some help before he hurt himself or anyone else. He was in what is called a psychosis state.[13] So, I immediately called 911. They arrived and found me still trying to calm Rodell down. After giving the paramedics his medical and psychiatric background, I agreed to the following: have him restrained in order to transport him to the nearest hospital, where he could be evaluated and if necessary, medicated and then admitted.

Upon arrival at the hospital he was rushed into a secluded room where a number of staff came to assist. Yes assist with a 12 year old who was still going through his psychotic breakdown and was pretty much giving each of us "the business". After several minutes with the paramedics, two nurses (one of which was a male) an ER physician along with myself, it was finally decided that he needed to be first placed in a straitjacket and then they were going to

---

[13] Psychosis refers to an abnormal condition of the mind and is a generic psychiatric term for a mental state often described as "involving a loss of contact with reality.

administer a small dose of Thorazine. Rodell was secured in the restraint system and given the dose of medication, however after about 30-45 minutes he was still in the same state of mind as he was when I first called the psychiatrist. He was still screaming and thrashing around as much as he could in the restraint, as if he had never been given anything to calm his aggressiveness at all. Labs were drawn to ensure there was nothing else medically going on in his body. Once those returned within normal limits, a second dose of Thorazine was ordered in an attempt to calm him down. This went on for several hours with no real results. It wasn't until the fourth dose that my son was calmed, trying to blow kisses, still wriggling his hands trying to get them free until he finally drifted off to sleep.

Once he was sound asleep, I was able to meet with the physician on call to discuss our next step or two. He informed me that he had just had a phone conference with Rodell's psychiatrist and that they were on the same page of admitting him to a facility in order to best observe him and make changes to his medications. I asked what were my other options and he just sighed and looked over at the bed Rodell was sleeping soundly in and said quietly, "you really don't have other options at this point because it appears he is outgrowing some of his meds." This was definitely something that I was not ready to do. So I gave him the negative on that option. However, I knew that we couldn't go on like this. The ER doc decided that he would give me the option of (even though he said there were no others) of increasing one of his psych meds. In doing so, he encouraged me to seriously think about placing him so they can make the changes in-house because he would need to be monitored. I agreed to think about it. Upon discharge he informed me that Roc's psychiatrist said I should contact his office in 2-3 days unless something changed. He also stated that they were going to work together with me to start the process of having him admitted somewhere, but this could take a while. He went on to explain that they needed to place him in a children's facility that had the room and the expertise, yet could also deal with his medical needs but most importantly be able to find a way to communicate with him while going through this ordeal.

Taking all of this information in, we left the hospital and arrived home. Rodell was still pretty much out of it (and truth be told, so was I) so sleep came relatively easy that night. Being mindful of saying a prayer of covering, I laid my head down and slept as peaceful as I could.

The next few days were uneventful. This was generally the case and I attributed it to yet again the increase in the dosage of the meds. School days were going by relatively easy also. Life as we lived it was peaceful.

The thing with being at peace in your life, there is always a trial or tribulation that precedes it or a storm that comes after. In this case I will say we were having our peace and the storm came at the tail end of it. This was a relatively big storm and it came out of nowhere and was in full effect, Rodell style.

Out of the blue one morning the fight began with what he wanted to wear to school. Per my usual I had already laid clothes out for the boys to wear the next day. The one thing that I had forgotten to do was to take the infamous blue thermal and the two sizes too small jeans with no button to fasten them, out of the dryer. I'm sure you have asked yourself why I had not just taken those things and tossed them a long time ago to alleviate having to fight over them.

Well it's just like with a small child and a security blanket or a favorite stuffed animal. These items were his security blankets. He felt comfortable in them and he looked for them every single day. Sometimes it worked while others it didn't. I kept them around knowing that it was one of those things that falls under choosing your battle to fight. However, this was not as an important battle as others.

On this particular day, Roc spotted his blue shirt in the dryer and went to get it. Before I had the opportunity to sneak and hide it, he had already opened the dryer door. Before I could walk over to where he was standing he had already slipped his shirt from over his head and was pulling the blue thermal over his head. I immediately started my negotiations of "let's save it for after school" and "ohhhh Rocky let mama see the shirt". He was not having it. He was clearly believing that he was wearing that shirt to school. As I walked over closer to him and attempted to take the shirt off while talking to him, he reached out and struck me. The fight was on. We went back and forth for a while. It wasn't too long after we started that the school bus came. By then, he was so tussled in his clothes that even if I had been able to calm him down, I would not have been able to redress him in time. So I left him sitting there, walked by him and grabbed up the swim shoes (because you know he found those also) and began to gather Rodney up so I could put him on the school bus.

It was my intention to get Rodell calmed down and then drive him to school myself. What I did not think was that while I was making my plans to take him to school, my son was in the house making his own plans to get his favorite items from me himself. I walked back into the house, Rodell was there waiting at the door for me crying. As he stood in front of me he tried to grab the items out of my hand. I moved my arms away from his reach and he tried again. I moved out of his reach and began to walk away. Before I knew it my son's fist had made contact with my back. In other words I was punched in my back with what I'm sure was all of his might. I quickly dropped the clothes and shoes and turned toward him only to find him coming at me like a freight train. I tell you that kid had prodigious strength. It was then that we began our tango of strength. I know you have also wondered why it seems as if I am repeating myself about our tussles. Well it is repetitive but each incident is more intense than the last. Hence, the reason for the increase of meds as well as my ability to realistically ward off his blows. On this day, one of his punches struck me so hard that I almost forgot that I had given birth to him. We went back and forth for what seemed like eternity before I could get him to calm down. There was even another individual involved (who shall remain nameless) that had much more strength than I and yet they were unable to hold Roc down for too long of a time. Out of breath I made what was at the time the most logical decision. I contacted his psychiatrist and once I was on the phone with him (at this point Rodell could be heard in the background screaming and banging his head continuously against the wall), I simply said to the doctor, "it's time". The doctor asked if I felt as if I could transport him to the emergency mental health building safely and I said I could. After receiving instructions on what to do and expect initially, I gathered him up and off we went to the emergency mental health.

During our time and after the hours of paperwork and attempting to speak to someone on duty who wasn't familiar with our case, I finally allowed Miss Trenny to come out in order to get some results. I had to advocate sternly about not placing my son somewhere that the professionals wanted to take him to in an ambulance and unaccompanied by me. That was not going to happen on my watch! I had to ensure that everyone knew that not only was he suffering from psychosis but he was non-verbal and didn't transition well, even at his baseline (normal) function. Once that was understood by all, and a few phone calls later, I was informed that a place had been located and a referral had been sent over. Directions were given to me and our three hour trip began.

At the facility, I sat in the car after driving around the parking lot a few times, attempting to get my emotions in check. As I looked in the back of my vehicle at my son who was now sleeping like a baby, I thought to myself that this has to be a trick of the enemy. I just knew that the young man I was looking at curled up on the back seat was not the same young man from a year ago. All I could say as a prayer before taking him into the facility was "peace be still."

Once inside, I met with the counselors and some staff. We sat and talked and they explained the rules and regulations of the facility and had me sign papers. They took me on a tour and explained to me about the doctor's orders and what to expect regarding Rodell's stay there at the facility and the minimum to maximum amount of time. There was one thing that was discussed that I had previously voiced my disagreement to with his psychiatrist. They were still insistent on the way to combat these psychotic meltdowns was to strip him off all of his medications and then start him on some new ones. Now under the circumstances I can see a physician instructing someone to stop taking a medication immediately. However, most of these medications are brain altering meds and if stopped abruptly they can lead to some serious issues such as seizures, hallucinations, etc. This is where I kept running into the stop signs. I just could not imagine doing something where the end result is supposed to be positive, and yet it was very likely to be just the opposite. Are you kidding me? So they wanted me to just throw my son under the bus like that? I again voiced my opinion and said that wasn't how I wanted to do things. I knew him and his body. I knew that he was very sensitive to any type of medicinal changes and that it could be a catastrophe. No I am not a doctor (well not certified anyway lol). However Dr. Mom I am. You see I have always stood strong in saying that I was thankful that God waited patiently for me to mature enough before He blessed me with the boys. He knew that I was going to have to handle a great deal. This great deal was to include the understanding and knowledge of medical issues, medicines, and the affects it can have on our bodies. So, sitting in a conference room with individuals from the medical/behavioral health field, I stood my ground and said, let's reconvene in the morning once the head physician of the facility was there to speak with us. All agreed and we focused on getting Rodell comfortable in his room. This also was not an easy task. He knew something was up but could not for the life of him figure it out. Not until it was time for me to make my exit. It was at that time, two of the residents had to restrain him. As I walked down the corridors I could hear his screaming. With each step I took, my heart hurt more and more. By the time I arrived back at the main door, I was a wreck. If you have ever had the opportunity to take your child to school on the 1st day of their educational journey and you felt as though you were abandoning them and felt as if you were the worse parent in the world as they screamed for you upon your exit....this was that scenario except amped up 1,000 times. Everything is always elevated with me and the boys because I always wondered how they would be able to speak up for themselves if they were in danger.

As I was sitting in the parking lot of the hotel where I was going to stay for the night, all of the anxieties and emotions paralyzed me. I could not move. I finally ventured off to get something to eat and to get my nerves together. I drove around the area, stopping at a few places. There was still something tugging at me about this place. I couldn't put my finger on it but it just didn't feel right. Then just as quickly as I couldn't figure it out, there it was, dropped in my spirit - - LoDebar[14]. Yes, this area reminded me of "not having" or "no pasture". In this very city I was about to leave my son, there was an overwhelming feeling of isolation and even destitution, if I may say so. I knew right then and there, even if I didn't have the uneasiness of a parent deserting their child, the understanding of evil spirits and how they can be dropped into your very soul[15] from what you surround yourself in was beating me up alone. I just, in good conscious could not allow my son to be left in that situation.

The next morning before the sun was up good, the doors of the facility were swinging open with me walking through them. Of course, I didn't give anyone a chance to say anything. I just said plain and simple, "I'm here to pick up my son." I refused to listen or much less hear anything that any one of the staff members had to say. I adamantly refused to allow him to stay there, stating "God did not give him to me for me to not be able to handle him. So, please release my son before we have some issues." They finally got the picture. It took a few hours for them to discharge him. However, once he was discharged, it was as if there was a party in our spirits. There was joy, love, kisses, laughter, hugs, more kisses and we left. The journey back to our city was uneventful, as were the next few days.

---

[14] "Lodebar: not having; no pasture." *2SAMUEL 9:1-13 (NIV)*
[15] 43 "When an impure spirit comes out of a person, it goes through arid places seeking rest and does not find it. 44 Then it says, 'I will return to the house I left.' 25 When it arrives, it finds the house swept clean and put in order. 45 Then it goes and takes seven other spirits more wicked than itself, and they go in and live there. And the final condition of that person is worse than the first." *Matthew 12:43-46 (NIV)*

We made it through the holidays with minimal outbursts. I continued administering the level of medications to him that was being prescribed prior to our attempt at placement at the facility. One of the medications, was discharged from his daily regimen in an attempt to alleviate the increase of sleepiness. It appeared after several weeks that there was a good therapeutic level of everything else that he was being prescribed.

We made it through the winter holidays and into the beginning of 2013. Rodell continued to have minimal setbacks in his behavior and meltdowns. His maturation level seemed to be growing daily. Then in February, my life was turned upside down.

Everyone in my household had come down with what appeared to be a winter cold. I kept both the boys in the house through the weekend and even an extra day on Monday (February 11, 2013) to ensure their cold symptoms were gone. The next day, with noses clear, fevers and coughing gone, I sent both boys to school. Excited to see the school bus pull up that morning, Rodney stopped doing his hand clapping and smiled and allowed the bus monitor to assist him up on the bus. Rodell was waving and saying "buhbye" and smiling and blowing kisses as he climbed up on the bus by himself. As the bus pulled off, I could still see his smiling face pressed up against the window, with him craning his neck the further along they drove until we could no longer see one another.

My day went on per usual. I had actually called the boys' school to speak with one of the administrators about another situation that I needed their assistance with. It was mid-morning, around 10:30 or so. The administrator mentioned during our conversation, that she had seen. Both boys and they looked well. She also mentioned to me that Rodell had fallen twice that morning. She explained that he was alright and had not injured himself. We both agreed that it was more than likely due to his normal level of clumsiness and left it at that.

Later that afternoon, approximately 2:30 as I was preparing myself for them to return home, I received a phone call. I looked at the number and frowned because I knew the number belonged to the bus dispatch from the special needs transportation department. I answered the call and was informed by the employee that the driver from the bus wanted me to meet the bus outside with Rodell's wheelchair. "Rodell's wheelchair?" I asked "for what?" I was then told they did not know, they were just conveying the message. I then said "Rodell does not have a wheelchair. Rodney does but it is kept at the school." Again I was told, the caller was just relaying the information. I thanked the caller and immediately went into panic mode. I knew something was going on. Confused, I explained the phone call to the individual there with me and we rushed outside to wait on the bus.

As the bus pulled up, I could see a face full of worry on the driver. We ran toward the bus and as the driver opened the doors he was shaking his head and said "they brought him to me like this". The driver explained to me that when Roc was wheeled out to the bus, he asked, "What's wrong with Roc? He looks like he is having a seizure or coming out of one." The individuals informed him that no he was not having a seizure and that "mom has been changing his medicines." However, "mom" had not been changing his medicines as of recent. The staff attempted, according to the driver, to lift Roc out of the wheelchair but he was unable to stand and was still "out of it". Again they attempted to bring him up the stairs to the bus, until the driver finally directed them to bring him to the back of the bus where he would be able to bring him up on the wheelchair lift. Once the driver finished giving his recall of the earlier conversation and events at the school, I ran up the bus stairs only to find Rodell, slumped over in the seat, against the window. I immediately could feel my heart beat in my throat. At first glance I knew my son was having a seizure. We removed him from the seatbelt and attempted to shake him and call his name. I lifted his eye lids to check his pupils. Felt his pulse and it was racing. His forehead did not signify a fever. I immediately started shouting orders out to the others that were around. I jumped off the bus and ran to get my vehicle all the while dialing for 911. As I pulled my vehicle close to the school bus, other residents were carefully bringing him from the bus to my truck. I opened the back door so they would be able to place him down on the seat while we waited for the paramedics. They arrived within a few minutes and quickly went to work. Their initial acknowledgment of seizure activity was made within the first minute. The paramedics asked me what seemed to be fifty million questions and I gave them fifty million and one answers. They inquired about his allergies in order to determine which medication they could give him to stop the seizure. Unfortunately, everything that was carried on the ambulance to administer for seizures, Rodell was allergic to. So placing him on oxygen and telling me to meet them at the hospital, they quickly drove off. I quickly gave brief instructions to Rodney's care giver and left to go to the hospital.

Generally, I have a really good recall of things that I have been through. However, to this day, I cannot remember how I made it to the hospital. Whether I ran any red lights, stop signs or had any near collisions. I just know that no sooner than I arrived, the registration nurses (both who knew me well from Rodney and all of his ER and/inpatient visits) saw me running through the entrance and they immediately sprang into action. They asked me the bare minimum questions in order to put his name in the computer (because the nurses from the back had already called to inform them that I was coming in). As we ran through the halls toward the back of the ER my head was pounding. I had all types of questions in my head and of course, with the way my thought process is set up, I was attempting to answer my own questions.

Upon entering the treatment area of the emergency room, one of the nurses gave me a quick side hug and said some encouraging words. As I walked into the room where I was told Rodell was, I found a scene that was familiar yet unfamiliar. It was familiar because I had become accustomed to being in this environment with all of this medical equipment but only with Rodney. It was unfamiliar because I had never been in this situation with Rodell. It's so different (not less important) when it's a child that has been going through emergent situations their entire life, as opposed to one who is rarely ever sick.

The medical staff didn't see me walk into the room because they were diligently working on him. There were several nurses, residents, doctors, clinical technicians, lab techs, you name it. Everyone was doing something. Asking for something. Passing something to someone else. The machines were hissing, pumping, buzzing, and ringing. There were sterile items being opened and the containers being tossed on the floor or toward the trash can. Syringes were being filled for multiple tubes of blood. Gauze pads, tape, blood pressure cuff, and all of this was being used simultaneously.

Unable to say anything I'm stuck and can't seem to open my mouth to make my presence known. I've seen this scenario. It was not good. It was hard to take in. Finally, one of the nurses sees me and shouts "mom is here". A doctor acknowledges my presence and says he will be right with me. In the meantime, another nurse comes in and makes room for me to sit across the room in a chair. I can see everything yet nothing at all. I notice my right leg is starting to shake a little. I suppose the clinical technician must have seen it too because as she is walking toward the trash can she stops beside me and says "I know you want your coffee. Give me a sec and I will get it for you." I look into her eyes and she gives me that "I know" look of empathy.

I look away as I hear a chair being dragged across the room. It's one of the physicians coming to sit down with me. As he leans in closer, some of the other medical staff shift places around the hospital bed and I get a better look at my son. I still at that point had not gone over to the bed. I felt like I was in a dream. That this scenario was just part of someone else's day and not mine. The last time I saw my son was on the bus peeping through the window with that silly, yet contagious grin he had, waving goodbye.

I turned my attention to the man sitting next to me as he calls my name. He begins by asking me can he get me anything. Once I shook my head no. He says in a gentle voice, "Tell me what happened to Rodell. Can you start from this morning when you last saw him?" I took a deep breath recalling our morning. I explained to the physician that I had just sent him back to school this morning after we had all been in the house with a bad cold over the weekend and keeping them both home an extra day to ensure they were no longer asymptomatic. I continued on telling him about how his energy level was back to his baseline and he was rambunctious and very bubbly and excited to be returning to school. I even went on to tell him how he said "get-get" and pointed to his radio (indicating that he wanted to take it to school with him) and how he for once did not throw a tantrum when I explained he had to leave it home so I could charge it and he could have it after school. It was then he interrupted me inquiring about the cold that we had over the weekend. I went down the list. No fevers. No vomiting. No diarrheas. Just a lot of runny noses and coughs that cleared up with some over the counter medications. He asked me whether anything happened at school and I explained the conversation I had with one of the administrators regarding Rodell falling twice. He asked if he had hit his head and I said not to my knowledge. I said the administrator informed me that both times he got right up and started walking again. I said that I didn't think anything of these two incidences because we all knew that Rodell could be quite clumsy at times. As far as I knew, I explained, the remainder of his day was normal.

It then it dawned on me at that very moment that because of the emergency, I had not been able to check for the daily email I should have received from his teacher informing me of what type of day Roc had. I asked the doctor to give me a quick second because I needed to see if anything else had happened at school to give us some answers as to what was going on with Rodell. I pulled out my phone and opened my email and sure enough there was my daily communication from his teacher. It indicated that he had fallen twice earlier in the day and was fine afterward. It went on to speak about his appetite and that he did not want to eat. Also in the email he was described as participating in his work for the day and earning his breads and reward time. Toward the end of the email, there was a narrative stating that "Rodell had a pretty rough day. He was very unstable and fell out of his chair a couple of times. He was in and out of sleep for the majority of the day. He was asleep for a solid two hours and unarousable at the end of the day and was twitching pretty badly in his sleep." I read this information to the doctor. I was shocked because remembering how I first saw him on the bus and looking at him now, I knew my son had been having seizures in school. The doctor immediately asked if Rodell had a history of seizures. I'm explained he had some absence seizures when he was a toddler, however he had been seizure free since and had never had the need to take any medication. The doctor then began to explain to me everything that was being done for treatment and the initial assessment is of course seizures. Due to the length of time (and we couldn't be sure at this point) how long he had been having seizures, they were finding it difficult to stop them. Several medications and dosages had not stopped the seizure activity so they had to place him in a medically-induced coma as well as intubate him with a breathing tube on the ventilator because his breaths were not adequate enough to open his lungs. In addition, his blood pressure had dropped so he was being provided medications to keep it up. He continued on to explain that they had drawn lots of blood in order to run various tests. Of course, he was going to ICU and once there and settled, they were going to schedule a 24-72 hour video EEG. This would possibly determine if how many seizures he was having, the duration of them and if he was having seizures that were not detectable by the eye.

As I stood up, several nurses were still standing around him working diligently. One nurse looked up and said, "We have him cleaned up now mom, you can come in and spend some time with him". I slowly walked closer to the bed. At the foot of his bed, I put my hand around his right foot and gave it a gentle squeeze and called his name. No response. Before I moved on, I gave it a second squeeze and as I did so, I said, "in the Mighty name of Jesus". I slowly continued up his body to his knee and right above at his thigh, I placed my hand on the most sensitive part (his tickle spot where I could always get a giggle from) and gave that also a gentle squeeze while saying "by His stripes he is healed". Being careful of all of the tubes draped over his torso and his right arm, I laid my hand in the middle of his chest and said "Jehovah Rapha we need you here". As the tears started to fall down my face, I'm trying to contain all of the negative thoughts that are going through my mind. The thoughts of hurt and harm toward others who I feel (and even to this day) that if they had acted accordingly, this may not have turned out as severe as it did. I wanted to see those that had him in their care and just send them back to Christ. Yes I wanted to get some "get-back" at my own hands. However, I quickly had to put those thoughts to the side for two reasons, one being I needed to focus all of my energy for whatever lay ahead for my son and myself; and secondly, I was a strong believer in what I was always taught about revenge.[16]

I leaned over and kissed my baby on his forehead. I touched his arm and realized how cold it was. She must have saw my expression because she said to me "it's because of all the IV fluids we have going into him. It has cooled his arm down." I looked at her and nodded my head. She continued to give me an update on his condition, his vitals, his seizure activity, meds being given and what to expect when he is taken upstairs to the Pediatric Intensive Care Unit (PICU). I explained to the nurse that I needed a few minutes to gather my thoughts and make a few phone calls before going upstairs. She said it was no problem and to take my time

---

[16] "Do not take revenge, my dear friends, but leave room for God's wrath, for it is written: it is mine to avenge; I will repay." *ROMANS 12:19 (NIV)*

because it may be a little while before we are called for a room and that she and another nurse were going to be in there at all times with him.

Once outside, I felt as if my legs were lead. I could barely walk. I found a bench right outside of the door and just kind of plopped down on it. My cell phone was in my hands and as I looked down on it, I realized the screen was soaked with water from my palms sweating. I just stared at it for a while and then placed my head down on my knees. My body rocked slowly back and forth until I was able to finally let my tears fall. I allowed the pain in my heart be just that. I needed to allow myself to go through these emotions and feel the torment of a helpless parent. This was one of those rare moments when I wanted to reach out to God and just tell him what I was feeling and what I wanted to not feel. However, the only thing I remember being able to say was nothing. It was then that my nothing turned into a small groan. Then then another one. Until finally a series of groans were bubbling up through my body and I knew that He was listening to me.[17] This was a process for me to go through not just to be able to cry, but once the crying was out, I could release it all and give it over to God. As long as I was holding on to the emotions that seemed to be engulfing my very being I would not be any good for myself or my son. I would not be able to understand what was going on and advocate for him if I was tied up in anger, fear and hurt. I had to release everything at that very moment. I did so, sitting right there on that bench, alone yet in the company of the Almighty.

---

[17] "In the same way, the Spirit helps us in our weakness. We do not know what we ought to pray for, but the Spirit himself intercedes for us through wordless groans." *Romans 8:26 (NIV)*

As I began to gather myself, I realized all the calls I needed to make. With each phone call I made, I seemed to get stronger in being able to give a clear description of what was going on. After a few minutes, I started my way back toward the ER where I clearly remembered my son laying there, with life beating breathed into him via machines and other instruments.

Shortly after I returned to his room, the ER physician and several nurses and techs appeared. The tech passing me all of his clothing he had on him upon arrival, registration requesting I sign here and there on the computer, while the doctor gave his last minute instructions. I was informed that a room in the Pediatric Intensive Care Unit was now ready and the team would be transporting him up. I knew from past experiences that this type of transport would require accuracy and speed. All of the machines that were not transferable had to be switched over to a portable one and the ones that were transferable would have to be carefully transported alongside of him. The preparation of everything took approximately an additional 15 minutes or so. We (a team of six and myself and Rodell) were then on our way.

The looks, the stares and the faces of empathy were seen throughout the halls of the hospital as we passed each one. This walk was beginning to feel as if everyone knew something that I did not know. Were they not telling me that he wasn't going to come out of this? Had the doctors and nurses not given me all the detailed prognosis as they should have? These were the questions bombarding my mind during our walk. It was then that I had to tell myself that these faces were God. That these thoughts and questions in my mind were opening the windows of my heart and trying to test my faith. We all know that the enemy comes to steal, kill and destroy. One thing that I learned in years past is that if the enemy can shake the foundation that holds a building together, then there is a good chance that the building would collapse. So I held my head up a tad bit higher. Squared my shoulders. Shifted my questions of doubt to the back of my mind and allowed my faith to be in the forefront of it all. As we boarded the elevator, I started to say the Lord's Prayer out loud, "Our Father, who are in heaven....." By the time all of us were snugly fit into, the elevator, I was at "forgive us our trespasses, as we forgive those....." The elevator came to a stop and we unloaded in the opposite manner. As I walked off at the rear of the elevator I (and now along with several of the staff with us) said together, "for thine is the kingdom, the power and the glory. Forever and ever. Amen". No one said anything else as we journeyed toward his room. That was enough. No questions. No comments. Just the peace of God.

Over the next few hours I watched the settling in process as well as the comings and goings of all assigned to the care of my son. I asked questions. Lots of them. I told the nurses to find the physician in charge of his care so I can speak to him. Eventually, the physician came in. We already had a rapport with one of another so he knew when I was ready to speak to him that it was going to be an all truth, no hold backs kind of conversation. This doctor knew from the past four or so years that I could handle whatever he told me and if I found it difficult that I would quickly go into prayer and come back with a new understanding of whatever information he had given me about what we were facing.

As we sat across from one another, cognizant of every swish, pump and beep of the machines that were continuously keeping Rodell in a state of living rest. We started the conversation rehashing over the events of the weekend and the cold issue. It was at that time that I found out that Rodell had tested positive for the flu, which would shed some light on the cold-like symptoms. We discussed the treatment for it. We went on to speak on his day at school that day. I allowed him to read the email I received from his teacher. When he reached the narrative about Rodell being asleep and twitching badly for the last two hours of school, he stopped, reread it out loud and then looked at me. I could tell he was thinking and choosing his words wisely. As he began to ask the ultimate question, "so he was seizing for two hours at the end of school?" I just nodded my head over and over again. He continued on by asking "they did not call you and tell you or call the paramedics?" I answered with "No. They called the nurse in and she said 'he's ok....mom has been changing meds'". [I am not including the name of the school, teachers, or administrators, city or state because they know who they are and the rest is up to God]. Do not take revenge, my dear friends, but leave room for God's wrath, for it is written: "It is mine to avenge; I will repay," says the Lord. (Romans 12:19 NIV). As we continued on, I explained what was provided to me via third party, again reiterating that no one from the school called to inform me of anything prior to him being released from school and sent home on the bus. It was at this point the two of us did the calculations and guesstimated that my son had been seizing for almost four hours prior to receiving any type of treatment in the emergency room.

We sat in silence for a minute or two. I then looked at the physician and asked him "what type of affect has this had on his brain?" He explained to me that generally when a patient has a seizure or a history of seizures, treatment is mandatory if the seizure lasts longer than five minutes. After five minutes, the patient is considered to be in 'status epilepticus'.[18] He went on to say that seizures can best be

---

[18] Status epilepticus is a potentially life-threatening condition in which a person either has an abnormally prolonged seizure or does not fully

described as a snowball being rolled down a hill. If you continue to roll the snowball down the hill, they will get bigger. However, the longer you allow the snowball to roll, it will get heavier and much more difficult to stop. In Rodell's case, after four hours, the staff at the hospital had a very difficult time stopping his seizures which is why he ended up being placed in the medically induced coma. The long term affects would not be known until they were able to control his seizures and he was no longer in need of the ventilator and medications to keep him stable. In other words, he had a long road ahead of him. The doctor discussed with me the route of treatment he was receiving now and what other options as far as medications that would be in the "next up" lineup. He suggested (as he always had in the past) that I allow myself some time for me while Rodell was in the ICU and to go home and rest while Rodney was in school. Of course, I knew that if anything changed, they would give me a call. I thanked him for his conversation and he left leaving me with a little more understanding of what I was seeing as I sat and looked at my son.

As the evening went on and family came and left, I decided to go outside for a walk. Entering the brisk night air, I allowed the days' events play out in my mind yet again. I had received a phone call from the school with apologies about what state Roc was in. Moreover, never once did I receive an apology from them not calling me and giving me the opportunity to either come get my son and take him to the hospital, nor why they had not called the paramedics themselves. I knew what I had to do. I had to confer with

---

regain consciousness between seizures. Although there is no strict definition for the time at which a seizure turns into status epilepticus, most physicians agree that any seizure lasting longer than 5 minutes should, for practical purposes, be treated as though it was status epilepticus.

legal representation. I would make sure that I placed that call the next day.

Up until that day, Rodell had always been such a healthy child. Nothing out of the ordinary or should I say outside of his baseline ordinary had ever been alarming. Even with his behaviors, they were difficult, yet they were not life threatening. As I walked, I prayed and talked to God. Unwinding my thoughts as I walked allowed the tension that had started to gather in my body to seep out slowly. I decided to not take the doctors' advice on this 1st night and go home. I wanted to be with my baby. My 12 year old baby. My "Baby Huey", my "Tubby", my "BamBam". Some of the nicknames we called him throughout his younger years. I just wanted to be in his presence. So I made my way back up to his room.

The night went on about the same as the day had. There were moments when a machine would beep and the nurse who was stationed outside his room would come in and make whatever adjustments needed. Early that morning Rodell's blood pressure spiked and an additional IV bag was hung and another line was added to the many lines already draping from poles to his bed, over his body. It was decided that a 24 hour video EEG would be hooked up to him. I had noticed that there was some intermittent shaking of one or more of his legs for short periods of time. I called the nurse in and we waited until she was able to see it for herself. While she was putting slight pressure on his leg (holding a limb to see if it will stop trembling is a way to determine if it's actually seizure activity), she also timed the activity. The nurse checked for his vitals, opened his eye lids to check his pupils and then left the room to page the doctor after these symptoms repeated themselves several times.

A few minutes later, the nurse returned with the physician as well as the on-call neurologist. They made their way around to Rodell's bedside and each looked, taking their turn examining him. They turned to me and asked me to describe to them what I had seen and how long I thought the duration of each episode was. I gave them an account of what I had seen and asked if he was still having seizures even in the medically induced coma. Yes. It sounded and appeared as if he was having some breakthrough seizures. The plan at that point called for a change in the dosage of two of the medications he was receiving in a slow drip to an increase of what is called a loading dose[19]. This was initially done in the ER but since the seizures appeared to be returning, the team decided to give him another loading dose, in hopes that it would stop the seizures. The medication appeared to have worked.

The next step was to have a 24 hour video EEG set up in order to determine if he was having some partial seizures. Partial seizures are produced (at least initially) by electrical impulses in a relatively small part of the brain. This test would also help the team determine whether these were partial, simple partial or complex partial seizures. Of course, by the time I was given the complete definition and an array of descriptions and possibilities my head was spinning. I was confused and scared. I was afraid of what the outcome would be. However, I immediately remembered what kind of God we (the boys and I) served.[20] So after saying a quick prayer, I was able to move forward with a clear mind without the distraction of fear and confusion.

---

[19] A large initial dose of a substance or series of such doses given to rapidly achieve a therapeutic concentration in the body.
[20] "For God hath not given us the spirit of fear; but of power, and of love, and of a sound mind." *2Timothy 1:7 (KJV)*

Over the next few days, there was evidence that showed Rodell was having a combination of seizures in the ICU. He was having clonic seizures[21] as well as tonic seizures[22]. Once this was determined the team met with me and once again medications were changed and dosages were increased.

After a few days the seizures appeared to stop. The team of physicians met with me again and said they wanted to try and turn down some of his levels of oxygen assistance and the ventilator to determine how much he could breathe on his own. I knew what was happening. They were not sure if my son was going to pull out of the state he was in. All I could remember was feeling as if someone had taken a larger than life vacuum and sucked all the air from the room. I could feel my shoulders tighten up as the nerves in my neck started to twitch. However, I immediately took control over all of these elevated senses in order not to fall prey to the stress my body was under. I had to be strong. This was not the time to get scared. I adjusted my body in the chair I was sitting in and looked each of the person in that conference room straight in the eye. As I made my glances around the room, I could feel my strength coming back to me. I then took a deep breath and said, "Most of you already know me. You know where my strength comes from and that I lean and believe totally on God." As the familiar faces started to nod in agreement, I continued by saying "I'm confident in knowing that whatever Gods will is, it will be done. So whatever it is that you feel should be the next step, do it." I went on to ask the expected questions (of which I already

---

[21] Clonic seizures: those that are repetitive, rhythmic jerks that involve both sides of the body at the same time. *(WEB MD)*
[22] Tonic seizures: those seizures that are characterized by stiffening of the muscles. *(WEB MD)*

knew the answers to but still needed to ask). We talked about what happens if once the ventilator is turned down what to expect. We discussed all of his vital signs and things the staff would be looking for and of course the deciding factor was if Rodell would still have seizures in the long run. There was no guarantee made from any of the physicians. There were some hopeful comments made and some words of encouragement given to me. Once I gave the go ahead to have his ventilator turned down, the team decided we would met back in his ICU room in a short while.

As I made my way back to Roc's room, I began to say a prayer in my head. I made it to his room and asked the nurse and the clinical technician if they would excuse themselves for a few minutes so I could have some time with him before the doctors arrive. When they were leaving I shut the sliding door and pulled the privacy curtain. I went over to my purse and pulled out my anointing oil. As I began to pray and thank God for His goodness, I anointed my son from the top of his head to the bottom of his feet. I dotted oil on the palms of his hands, his chest and his legs. I touched every single part of his body that I could reach without disturbing any of the many tubes running everywhere. The last thing I did was to lean over and kiss my son on his head before the tears just began to flow. In between the tears I continued to bless God and thank Him for bringing us as far as He had. I thanked Him for preparing me for this by allowing me to be a more mature individual. I petitioned Him for the healing that I knew only He could provide at this point. It was then, the team knocked on the glass as they slid the door open and started to congregate in the room.

I stood up straight and cleaned my face off as we all acknowledged one another again. As each one of the specialists and a few nurses gathered around the bed into

115

their prospective places. There was a level of high intensity in the room. The head physician barked out orders of pushing more of different medications through his IV lines. As he started to adjust the knobs on the ventilator the beeps on the machine seemed to get louder (I think this was just my anxiety building again). All eyes kept going back and forth from the ventilator to Rodell to computer screen showing all of his vitals. Each one of us was silent at that point just waiting to see if anything of an emergent situation would show up. After about five minutes, there appeared to be a collective sigh of relief in the room. The doctors started to each give their count of what they believed to be his state at that time. He appeared to be holding his own at the new levels of assistance. There were no new signs of seizures and his pulse ox was still steady. His blood pressure was stable. Rodell, my youngest, my baby boy was still there! Hallelujah.....God was not ready for him yet. Before I could ask anything, the head physician stated that the machines would be kept at these new levels and that blood gases would be drawn periodically to ensure his true oxygen and carbon dioxide levels known. After the next twelve hours (if there were no incidences), they would reconvene and determine if the levels of assistance could be turned down even further. A few more adjustments to his orders were given to the nursing staff as the team of physicians departed.

Left in the room with a clinical technician and a nurse, I could do nothing but smile. Even though my son was still unresponsive and there at least 15 different tubes running into his body, I knew it wasn't over and that in itself was enough to make me push on with the joy that God was still in control.

In the next week Rodell was extubated from the ventilator and some of the IV lines were discontinued. The hours after the ventilator was turned off were very nerve wrecking, since the machine was no longer breathing for him. However, he was still on the nasal cannula for oxygen for slight support. That evening as I was sitting in the hospital room, I heard a slight rustling sound. I glanced up from my iPad and looked around the room. I didn't see anything or anyone so I went back to reading. Approximately 10 minutes later the clinical technician came back in the room to sit with us. We chatted a few minutes about his status. Then the rustling sound came back again. We looked at one another, both of us asking had the other heard the noise. We turned from where we were sitting at looked over toward Rodell and the sound came again. Our attention immediately went to the bottom of the bed. It was his legs under the sheets. He was moving his legs around. He was waking up. The tech ran out of the room to go get someone. I jolted to the bed and grabbed his little hand and started to massage it. As I called his name, and encouraged him to listen to my voice and open his eyes, the movement of his legs started to occur more frequent. All of a sudden his eyes popped open and I just cried like a big baby. All I could do was to let his hand go and walk around the room giving God praise. I quickly gathered myself and went back to his bed and in that quick moment I was the recipient of RadioRoc's little quirky smile. My heart just melted right then and there. I was in love with my baby boy more than the first day of his life. That's how I felt. That moment when you give birth and you see your newborns face for the very first time and you just melt on the inside and fall in love. Yes. That's what I felt at that moment.

I watched him as he looked around the room. Trying to move his arms and his legs all at the same time. He noticed all of the tubes and immediately tried to reach for them. He knew they weren't supposed to be there. He knew he had always tried to take them out of his big brother's arms when he would visit him in the hospital. As the tech and the nurse

117

came rushing in, they noticed that he was reaching for the tubes. We were asked by the nurse to hold each arm to keep him from pulling on the lines while she ran to get the doctor paged.

That evening proved to be uneventful with any negative changes in Rodell's condition. After the doctors assessed him and ordered to have some soft restraints for his arms and legs to keep him still. These restraints were used on the boys because of their aggressive behaviors and to keep them from pulling out their IV lines. While Rodell was on the ventilator, all of his psychotropic medications had been discontinued. There was no need for them while he was not up and about. However, without them, it would be a task to keep him not only from being aggressive the more awake he became but also to keep him (and us) safe.

Everyone was overjoyed as the word started to spread around the unit. Heads of various staff members started to peek in his door either with encouraging words or just to flirt with him and see that smile of his. There were still a few breakthrough seizures each day that passed, but again adjustments to his dosages generally stopped them. The day arrived to take him off oxygen. Well let's just say the day came when he actually wriggled one of his hands from a restraint and he removed the nasal cannula himself. This was his way of saying enough already, I'm ready and I'm running this show. Once removed, the doctor was called in to assess him yet again and agreed with Rodell it was time to remove him from the oxygen.

After a few days of breathing on room air and slowly being introduced back to foods and being able to be wheeled around to the different nursing stations, his team of physicians decided it was time for him to go home. Now going home was exciting however, there was a big catch. It appeared that since his admission several weeks prior with the initial seizures, and the length of time he had seizures without treatment on February 12, there were some lasting affects it had on his abilities. With the oxygen deprivation, one of the things discussed was the fact that we would not know whether or not there would be any loss of skills or any brain damage until later. Well later was here. We found that he could no longer sit up straight. He was always slumped or leaning over to the side. Very similar to a stroke patient that loses their strength on one side. There was also his ability to stand and walk. Now this skill was one that was figured to come back later because he had been in the hospital bed for several weeks so naturally, this wasn't as alarming. Then there was his speech. Everyone knew that Rodell had his way of talking, even with his limited vocabulary. However, his limited vocabulary had now become very limited. He was pointing a great deal more than he had before. Even though he was pointing, he pointed with a smile and with confidence. He definitely had found his way of being able to get his point across. This lack of communication was not going to deter this strong little boy from being heard. He was definitely my son.

So the day comes for his discharge. We leave with a number of new instructions, medications, appointments and referrals. As I push him down the hall in the wheelchair and we say our thank you's and buhbye (in Rodell's voice), I leave a little more worn out, rejuvenated but most important, grateful. Thankful that even though there is a new level of care needed for my son and that means more for me to do, I was thankful that God has kept me through it all in order to do it.[23]

Over the next week or so, there are a few attempts of sending Roc back to school. There actually was not one full school day completed. He would arrive to school just fine, after having a seizure free night and morning, only to have them during the school day. I was having to pick him up every day from school. Once I relayed this information to his neurologist, yet another change in the dosing and times of his seizure medications were made. This was done in an effort to try and control them more during what was appearing to be a "peak time" or "pattern of episodes".

The seizures would always stop during the first few days of dosage or medication change, even to include additions added to his daily regimen. During the times where he was able to stay away for several hours (because most of the new dosing and medications made him sleepy), I would have him propped up in a wheelchair. He showed no signs of his ability to sit up of improving. Pillows between his body and the wheelchair to provide a cushion, along with a belt or two holding around his trunk and waist to hold his body secure to the wheelchair. It was also at this time, that he could no longer stand to take the showers that he had just recently before the seizures began to enjoy. I had to revert back to giving him a bath. Even during the bath times, Rodell could no longer sit up, so someone had to always be present in order to bathe him. Most days there needed to be at least two of us present, due to the fact that he had also started having seizures in the bath tub.

---

[23] "Cast your cares on the Lord and he will sustain you; he will never let the righteous be shaken." *Psalm 55:22 (NIV)*

One afternoon, in early April, his seizures started up and even with the emergency medication I had to dispense, they just would not stop. So naturally, the paramedics were called and he ended up back in the hospital. In the emergency room, it was not as intense as his original hospital stay was, but because of the severity of a seizure things were still very detailed. Naturally, he ended up being admitted because the seizures still were resistant to medications in the ER. During this stay, the team, huddled, planned, ran labs, performed another video EEG, brain scans, you name it. The diligence that was provided to his care was superb from a medical standpoint. With every physician, resident, neurologist, nurse, et al. that was assigned to his care, one would think that someone would end up finding some type of medication that would control his seizures. Again, after much revision to his medication regimen, the seizures seemed to be under control and after about a week or so, Roc was discharged to go home again. A few pounds lighter, muscle tone not as strong as when he was admitted, however, that smile was still there. We left and went on that familiar walk down the hall giving out hugs of gratitude to the staff. Once home, I realized that this could very well be a scenario that may go on for a good while before the medical staff found a combination of medications for him. Over the next few weeks, there were two more additional hospital admissions for his seizures with the outcome of each being the same, except for the last one. This was the one at the end of April. His neurologist had completed his assessment in his room and we sat down to talk. It was then that he informed me that he was diagnosing Rodell with Lennox-Gastaut Syndrome (LGS)[24]. He went on to explain to me what LGS was and the effects it could bring (and appeared to already be bringing) to Rodell's life. He paused, looked me straight in the eye and then said "it is debilitating and life-threatening". Did someone just suck the air out of the room again? My God is all I could say. The neurologist went on to explain that when diagnosed with LGS a different level of FDA approved medications for seizures would now be open to prescribe to him. Advising me that there was no "fix' for the syndrome nor a medication that would stop his seizures altogether. I sat back in my chair and asked "so this means his seizures will never get better and all of his skills that we have worked on over the last 12 years will never be regained?" His answer was a simple, "I'm afraid so." The best thing we can focus on would be providing him with the best quality of life we can give him in between the seizures." We chatted more about the assistance I would need in my

---

[24] Lennox-Gastaut Syndrome (LGS) is a rare and often debilitating form of childhood-onset epilepsy. The syndrome is characterized by a triad of signs including multiple seizure types, moderate to severe cognitive impairment, and an abnormal EEG with slow spike-wave complexes. This triad of mixed seizures, abnormal EEG and intellectual impairment represents one of the most difficult forms of epilepsy to treat. LGS is also a physically dangerous epilepsy syndrome of childhood because of the frequent falls, injuries, and cognitive impairment that can severely limit quality of life. In 20-30 percent of cases, no cause can be found. Many children are typically developing normal when first diagnosed, but then begin to lose skills, sometimes dramatically, in association with uncontrolled seizures. Young children with LGS may exhibit behavioral issues, personality disturbances, mood instability, and slowing of psychomotor development. Behavioral disturbances can include poor social skills and attention seeking behavior, which can be caused by the effects of the medication, difficulty interpreting information, or due to continued electrical disturbances in the brain. Some children with LGS are prone to develop non-convulsive status epilepticus (a continuous seizure state that is associated with a change in the child's level of awareness). This requires medical intervention to bring it to an end.
(www.lgsfoundation.org)

day to day life for him as well as the medications and the approval process for insurance coverage. He decided that he would keep him in the hospital for another 3-5 days in order to ensure that medications would be approved quicker. I agreed. That was a big blow. This was a pretty big for me to swallow. Think of a child who is an athlete, possibly a football player. You go to their games and practices, watching them gain their skill level and progress with each season. One day out of the blue, your child is playing a game and as he is running down the field, he gets hit so hard he flies up in the air. He lands, and doesn't get up, ends up injured for life and you have to take care of them from that point on. That's what I was feeling at that moment. I knew at that point that everything he had trained for, worked hard for, and was taught, was no longer going to be a part of his day to day life. However, as his mother, it was my love that was kicking into a higher gear to ensure that whatever he had lost and would never gain back, he would not feel the despair of missing out on it. I would continue to be his mouthpiece and speak for him. My legs would be the strength to walk with him while I held him up. He could sit up as straight as he possibly could, because I would sit next to him and be his back to hold him up. That was my promise to him, myself and God.

By the time he was discharged and home over the next few days, the seizures were almost an ongoing occurrence around the clock. He was having upwards of 25, 50 & 75 per day. Some days maybe more because he was still having the smaller ones that lasted only seconds or that we were not able to see. His seizures were so often (and sometimes scary) that I started sleeping with him. I did this for two reasons. One was so that I could hear any type of struggle he may have in the middle of the night. Secondly, I just did not want him to have the feeling that he was in this alone. He needed me, but I needed him more.

Approximately three weeks after the diagnosis of LGS, I awoke a little earlier than my normal time. However, I didn't just wake up. I was startled in my sleep. I knew as soon as I opened my eyes what was going on. I screamed before I could even jump over the bed and turn the light on. I don't even remember firing off orders for the paramedics to be called, I just know that in that quick instance, as I threw the covers off of my son, I heard that rough, rattling sound I knew to be the sound of someone struggling for their last breaths. As I fell to my knees and looked at him screaming his name and propping his head up with my hand I saw that he had already started turning colors. His face, neck, even his tongue was purple. A dark purple. I knew already, what we were facing.

The paramedics arrived and took one look at him. They pushed me out of the way and ripped his little white t-shirt open to look at his chest. They sprang into action so fast with one EMT grabbing the bottom of his head and the other his feet and dragging him across the bed and right out of the door. All I remember hearing was 'guppy breaths', 'oxygen', 'meet us there'. I was in a frenzy. I knew from being around life and death what I had just witnessed when I opened my eyes. I also knew what the words "guppy breath" meant. So in an adrenaline rushed state, I threw some clothes on and grabbed my keys and purse and flew to the hospital.

Upon my arrival, I didn't even go to the parking garage. I pulled up at the emergency entrance and tossed the keys to my truck and pretty much snatched the parking ticket from the courtesy clerk. As I ran into the hospital, the triage nurses looked up and just as three months prior they recognized me and ushered me immediately to the back. The only difference with this occasion, I believe they knew ahead of time that the scenario with Rodell in the back was much more emergent than before because they didn't make me stop to get a visitors sticker.

After a quick power walk to the emergency room, I was stopped at the nursing station. The nurse who stopped me explained that the staff was still working on Rodell and asked me to sit outside of the room. I hesitated but obliged. As I sat there with my heart racing, my eyes darting all around trying to settle my thoughts down. One of the clinical technicians that was familiar to me came and offered me a cup of coffee, a bottle of water and a handful of tissue (I hadn't even realized tears were falling from my eyes). She didn't say anything. Just offered a half smile and a squeeze on my shoulder. What seemed to be an eternity went by and finally a nurse came to get me to escort me into the emergency room where Rodell was.

Upon entering the room, I felt a chill. As I placed my belongings down, I took a mental note that this was an almost identical scenario to February 12, just a few days short of 90 days prior. Some of the staff was still scurrying around attending to him, hooking up IV lines, setting the alarms on the monitors, and a host of other things. I knew at that very moment, that my son was not there. His body was there, but he wasn't. Several familiar physicians walked up to me and pulled some chairs up and motioned for me to take a seat with them. They began with telling me how sorry they were to have to see us again and that Rodell was having such a hard time. The conversation continued on with them asking me about the morning's events. I explained, starting from the night before informing them of the seizures he had that evening up until the breaths that I heard when I opened my eyes.

In dealing with me and the boys from the many hospital visits, the staff there knew that I was a straight from the hip kind of parent. So they began by telling me, that of course, he was on life support. The ventilator was doing all of the breathing for him at this point, he was being given a loading dose of seizure medications, medications to stabilize his blood pressure and they had already taken multiple tubes of blood in order to run more tests. Naturally, they were waiting for room in the ICU and explained that it could be a while because it was crowded. I looked them in the eyes and asked, "It's not good is it?" Being careful not to speak outside of the gray area, one of the physicians says, "This is a bit more critical than his admission in February." With that said, they asked if I needed anything or needed to go make calls to my relatives. I said, "Yes I do." One of the physicians replied, "We still have a few more things to wrap up in here and the nursing staff will remain with him, so go and take all the time you need."

I walked over to the bed and squeezed his foot and proceeded to his head and kissed his forehead. I said to him, "hang in there baby boy." I walked outside to make some calls to family members and close friends explaining to them what happened. Each agreed again, to come up and sit with me. It was times such as this, I don't believe my family and close friends knew how much support I really needed. More than they could ever imagine.

I made my way back to his room. By then, most of the medical staff had left and it was only two nurses and a clinical technician remaining. One of the nurses pulled up a

126

chair on the opposite side of his bed so I could sit with him. I made myself as comfortable as I could and sat down. I reached up onto his bed and found his little stubby fingers half curled and slid a few of my fingers inside and sat there. Waiting patiently and praying.

It was several hours before an ICU room was available. Once upstairs the staff was already in the room waiting for him. There were again some familiar faces. A few of those individuals walked up and gave me little quick hugs. There was kind of an unsaid conversation going on in the room. Albeit, the machines were beeping, the ventilator was swooshing and pumping air into his lungs, I believe each of us knew that the remnants of my son's life was very little.

With this being such a duplication of recent events, the nursing staff spoke to me and briefed me on everything that was going on with Rodell. While talking with them, several doctors stepped into his room. They asked me if wanted to talk there or in a conference room. I said no I'm good here. One of the doctor's motioned for me to sit down. I declined. In the ICU I had a pretty decent rapport with the staff. However, on this day, I wanted to direct my attention to one of the physicians that I had known and dealt with over the last few years. I locked in on their eyes and said, "What now?" The physician began to give me the long list of things that Roc was dealing with. Starting with his struggles for breath when the paramedics arrived, which as I thought, were the end-of-life breaths. They went on to explain that all of his seizure medications were increased and were being given through the IVs. In addition, he was being given medication to keep his blood pressure up. His blood pressure was extremely low and he was also being kept warm with multiple blankets strategically placed around his body. I glanced over to where he was in his bed and knew I had to ask the ultimate question. "Is this the end for him?" One of the physicians stated that they would not be sure of anything this early on and at such a critical state. However, with all that he had going on, he had a big fight ahead of him. I knew the doctors could not tell me what we all kind of knew already. So I just looked at them and, "Well we already know he is a fighter." They agreed and stated they would be right outside of his room or in short distance away if I needed anything or had any other questions.

During the rest of the day, visitors came, sat, cried, talked, told funny stories about him and supported me. Once every one had left, I went out for one of my walks again to clear my head. As I walked, I talked to God and just told him "thank you" for all that he has done. I told God, "Just as you prepared me before I gave birth to these boys; please prepare me for when you decide to take him home with you." The thing that I have always stood by is having a direct conversation with God. He already knows our hearts and our thoughts. However, it's when we speak things to Him in acknowledgement of our trials, He loves that we are in tune and understanding of what is going on.

The next morning, Friday, nothing had changed. There were some tests done through blood word to determine how much if any breathing Roc was doing over or under the ventilator. The results were that he was doing very little under the ventilator. This meant that the ventilator was doing most of the breathing for him. There was a setback that indicated he had some blood in his lungs and upon testing and x-rays, those tests were positive. With this condition, it also showed his lungs were not opening up enough (one was already collapsed). This condition called for a more intense breathing support system. So he was removed from the ventilator and placed on the Bilevel Positive Airway

Pressure[25] (BiPAP) machine. This would be used to hopefully open his lungs up more, In addition, with the respiratory distress he was found in Thursday morning there was also a possibility for more brain damage because of the lack of oxygen. Everything that had happened previously was in an elevated status with this hospital admission. Throughout the day there were alarms that went off from time to time, but other than that, there were no major positive changes.

Saturday came and visitors stopped by, calls were made, hugs were given, but no signs of anything or anyone being able to tell me anything different. I had several conferences throughout the day with the physicians giving me their brief updates. It was at this point I felt as if I were just walking in a zombie state. It was Mother's Day weekend and all things considered, I truly did not feel like celebrating. It was late afternoon and a nurse was in the room attending to some of his needs. We were having idle chit chat about the holiday coming up. I looked up at her and asked "My baby isn't coming back is he?" She looked away and said "Oh well I have seen lots of children bounce back. You know kids are resilient." I agreed. However, I just knew in my heart of hearts that what I said was true.

Later that night, I decided I would go home and try and get some rest and prepare myself to come back the next day. As I was driving down the dark main road toward home. I decided not to turn on any music. I wanted to ride in silence and rest my brain a little. As I'm sitting at a stop light at approximately 11:30 I hear a voice. It says, "I'm taking Him

---

[25] BiPAP can be described as a continuous positive airway pressure system with a time-cycled or flow-cycled change of the applied pressure level used for acute/chronic respiratory failure.

home. He's going to be too difficult for you to take care of."
I knew the voice. It was the Holy Spirit.[26] Now even though
I have my own relationship with Christ, it is still in some
instances a little disturbing to hear a voice and you know you
are alone. There was no one else in the vehicle with me.
There were no other cars on the dark road or at the light
beside me. I looked around in my car to make sure I was in
deed in my own vehicle alone. I was. It was at that point, I
knew it was God's will being spoken to me. Now in times
when we hear our direction from the Holy Spirit, we may
attempt to ignore or pretend we didn't heart it. However, in
this instance, I knew what it was and was thankful that it was
being conveyed to me in the way it was. All I could do was
say "thank you Jesus." Not just thank you for what was just
told to me. I was saying thank you because He thought
enough of me to honor my petition of "God please prepare
me for when you are ready to take him home." This was my
preparation. My advance notice so I could be ready. As
ready as a mother could be. I was thankful that even in my
love for my son as a mother, I did not want to see him suffer
and become what I knew God hadn't placed him here on
earth to be. So I said thank you. Again. Again. Again and
again!!!! The tears streamed down my face as I continued
driving and I just thanked God for Rodell's life. For the
rarity of his syndrome. For the trials and the triumphs. I
thanked him for the lives that Rodell was able to touch. I
just thanked Him all the way home.

Once home, I sat in the truck to get myself together. I knew
I had to because there were people that would need me to be
their support system upon hearing the update on Rodell. I
know you are saying why would I need to be their support
system when I am losing my son? That's just the God in me.

---

[26] "But when he, the Spirit of truth, comes, he will guide you into all
the truth. He will not speak on his own; he will speak only what he
hears, and he will tell you what is yet to come." *John 16:13*

130

He made me that way, blessed with strength and endurance. I slowly made my way into the house. I looked around and went straight to Rodney. I knelt down by his bed and gave him a few kisses on his cheek and forehead. I reached up to his hair and rubbed his locs and told him that I loved him.

It was late and I knew I needed some rest. So I quickly prepared myself for bed, said my prayers and laid down. Of course I wasn't sleepy. Tired, yes. Exhausted, absolutely. However, as in most stressful cases, I couldn't fall asleep. I just laid in the bed staring at the ceiling for all of an hour until I finally started to unwind and then eventually fell asleep.

The next day, I got up and called the hospital to make sure there had been no changes. Outside of Roc's blood pressure and his body temperature (which was now hot because he had a fever), everything else was still the same. The nurse informed me that some labs had in fact come back indicating that he was harvesting some type of infection and they had started him on IV antibiotics. She also informed me that respiratory therapy had come in and attempted to turn his levels down on the BiPAP machine to see how he would do and that did not work so well. As well as an additional x-ray still showed signs of the collapsed lung not opening up. I explained to her that since it was Mother's Day I wanted to run a few quick errands and I would be there in a few hours. She stated she would call me if anything occurred that needed my attention or permission to treat.

I took the next few hours to spend time with Rodney, love on him and also to see a couple of family members. I made phone calls and tried to relay information to a few relatives out of the area to no avail. I also took the time to contact some of his care attendants in Charlotte, NC to give them updates on him. By mid-afternoon I decided to make my way to the hospital. I had also told a few family members to meet me their if possible.

Entering into his ICU room was harder on this day than any other day. The first thing I thought of when I saw him was what the Holy Spirit had revealed to me the night before. This made me have all types of emotions to flood in. Secondly, as I looked at his face, it appeared to be more swollen than it was the previous day. When all of the fluids are being pushed into someone who is not moving around enough to void or burn it off, then it sits stagnant in your body. I leaned over and gave my baby a kiss, squeezed his hand and talked to him for a little while. As some visitors started to arrive, I explained to them that I needed to talk to them. I filled them in on the conversation that I had the previous day with some of the physicians about Living Will for him and whether or not to sign a Do Not Resuscitate order. This was a very difficult conversation for me to talk about as well as those that were close to me to hear and accept. Questions were asked and answered and opinions were given. The end result was pretty much supporting my decision on whatever I decided to do. We continued to visit a while longer, each of us taking turns to going back and forth in the room. At the suggestion of everyone, including the medical staff, to go home and get some sleep, I decided to do so a few hours after all of the visitors had left. So again around midnight after saying good night to Rodell, I kissed him on the forehead and said "luhluh" and left to go home.

I had been sleep for approximately four hours and my phone rang. I jumped straight up and answered it before it could sound a second time. It was the hospital. The head physician was on the other line explaining to me that they have all medications to the maximum levels and dosages they can give to Rodell and yet he still was not doing well. I needed to come and I needed to call my family is what was told to me. I hung the phone and quickly got dressed. I didn't want to call anyone just yet. I needed to get there first, talk to the staff in person, and then I would contact my family.

I rushed to the hospital and ran through the halls until I arrived at his room. As I went around the partially closed curtain I could feel my heartbeat in my throat, ears and on my temples. Inside the room there were several doctors and nurses attending to him in one form or another. I made my way to his bedside and felt his hand, it was cool. I looked at all of the numbers on the monitors and realized some were extremely high while others were very low. I inquired about the numbers and was informed that the blood pressure medication given to him to keep his pressure up was no longer working. It was at its maximum level and it would not be much longer. They would be able to hold it there as long as I needed or desired to, however, there was nothing else they could do for him. The BiPAP machine was working extremely hard in pushing the air in and out of his lungs but I was told that the movement I saw in his chest was pretty much all of the machine working. His heart rate was extremely low and I already knew from being in rooms of family members that were dying, that the rate was at a very crucial point. Again, they said they could hold him as long as possible, however, they recommended I contact my family. They inquired as to how I wanted to proceed with the end of life with him. Options presented to me were to either turn all machines off at once to allow him to slowly transition; or they could slowly turn the machines down and allow us to stay in with him until his transition is complete. I was stunned. I was unable to move for a few seconds. In knowing the reality of a situation as death is one thing. However, facing it head on in those last moments is totally different. I let out a gasp and then the tears flowed. I needed time. I wanted to beg for more time. However, I knew that would not be fair to him. The Rodell who I had grown to love and cherish was since long gone and to keep him here with me in this state was unfair. I hugged and kissed him and whispered "luhluh" in his ear and ran my fingers through his little curls on top of his head. I looked up at the doctors who were standing there and said, "Let's do it slowly once my family arrives." They agreed. The social worker came in and we went over and signed paperwork. I asked them to allow me to contact my family. They agreed again.

I made the necessary calls to my family members and close friends. I asked each one of them if they wanted to be present during the time of transition and if they wanted to come and say their final farewells. Naturally, each phone call I made contained tears from both sides of the phone and ended with each person saying "I'm on my way now."

While I waited in the hospital room, I became fidgety. I moved things around. I restacked supplies. I stood up beside him. I sat down in a chair. I was all over the place. Finally, my family started arriving. Even his comrade. His partner in crime. His shadow. His big brother Rodney. We bought him close to the bed and allowed him to stand close and touch him. He looked Rodell directly in the face, something that he rarely did and made a sound that was kinship to him saying "hi".

Before I knew it, the staff was beginning to congregate in the room and outside the door of his room. They all came in to pay their respects to him as well as us. There were lots of tears and of course hugs from all. Words of encouragement came from the physicians that explained how proud they were to have been able to be a part of Rodell's life along with words of how they were fascinated by my strength, courage, dedication, and faith. I thanked each one of them for all of their efforts and outstanding care they had provided to my son.

There was a prayer said at that point. A prayer thanking God for Rodell Miles Nelson's life. A prayer of protection for his soul during his transition. It was very overwhelming to all. There was not a dry eye anywhere. After the prayer was done, the physician asked if I wanted to get in the bed with him. I did. All of the tubes and lines were moved around so I could climb up beside him. I draped my arm over his chest and curled up in a fetal-like position next to him. Next, I did the only thing I knew to do. I sang to him. The song that I had sung to each of them at any trying time in their lives. I sang "Jesus loves me; this I know. For the bible, tells me so. Little ones, to Him belong. For they are weak, but He is strong. Yes. Jesus loves me. Yes. Jesus loves me. Oh yes. Jesus loves me. For the bible tells me so."

At the end of the song, I looked at my son and said how much I loved him and how much of an honor it was to be his mother. I told him how proud I was of him and his strength. I told him not to be scared and that he could go to Hallelujah (what he called church) all the time now. I gave him a kiss and through my tears I said "Luhluh Rodell. See you soon."

I turned my attention from his face toward the doctor and we nodded at one another. It was then that he started to turn the machines down. Each machine that was breathing life into my son. Each machine that was keeping my baby's seizures at bay. Each machine that was keeping Roc's blood pressure up. Each machine that was keeping Rodell from going from his labor to his eternal rest.

135

Rodell Miles Nelson transitioned to life everlasting on May 12, 2013. You will always be a big part of our hearts. We love and miss you RadioRoc.

RODNEY PREPARES TO GO HOME

Rodney has always been my medically fragile child. He has had many obstacles to overcome from day one. As I have stated previously, in the first 10 years or so of his life he was in the hospital on an average of every six to eight weeks. There were the times when his illness may have not required a hospital admission, but he was still at home sick. More often times than not, a common cold would turn into acute bronchitis or pneumonia. If I had to guess, I would say that he has been diagnosed with pneumonia at least 25 times in his life.

I can recall a time when he was much younger and he was diagnosed with pneumonia. The doctors at that time were attempting to treat him as an atypical child and assumed that he could go home and rest, and take lots of fluids and bounce right back. I argued that this was not the case with him and that he would require IV fluids and a strong antibiotic. The attending physician at the ER at the time thought I was being an overprotective mother and insisted I follow his instructions and that he would be ok. We went back and forth with our opinions and he would not give in. He stated that Rodney should be back to his medical baseline[27] in about five to ten days. I gave in (something that is very hard for me to do) and took my sick child home to nurse on him myself. After about a week or so, there was no marked improvement in any of his symptoms. I ended up taking him back to his pediatrician and explained to her what had been said at the ER. After his doctor did an assessment on him, the end result was to take him back to the hospital. The only difference this time, was a phone call was placed to the

---

[27] Information that is used as a starting point by which to compare other information (medical). (Merriam-Webster)

hospital making prior arrangements for him to be admitted and treated. Once admitted in the hospital, Rodney received another x-ray which showed his pneumonia had become worse. Due to his body's inability to fight most things off, coupled with his severe reflux (which causes his gastric juices to flow upwards), his pneumonia landed him in the ICU. Of course, I was furious and wanted to take someone's head off. However, a lesson such as this was added to my soap box which I would later learn to stand on when advocating for him.

It was in the hospital stay in 2006 that the medical staff realized there may be something else that was constantly causing him to have pneumonia so often. There was a test done called an Upper Gastrointestinal Endoscopy (Upper GI)[28]. The results of the test revealed that he had a chronic case of Gastroesophageal Reflux Disease (GERD). Most of us either have dealt with reflux ourselves or have someone in our family who suffers with it or severe cases of heartburn. GERD is generally treated with a change in eating habits. However, he was already on a diet of baby foods, oatmeal, fig newtons, and whatever other foods I could mash, smash or even pre-chew for him (sorry that's what mother's do for their babies). Since his diet wasn't able to be modified too much more, the doctors decided to add a prescription for it. An adult strength medication given twice daily was supposed to help him tolerate his foods and not be in as much discomfort. I guess you are wondering, how does pneumonia and GERD go together. Well think about when you are eating, you choke and it comes back up. Most of us have the ability to be able to dislodge whatever it is we are choking on. Rodney was not able to do that. If he choked (in addition to his challenge of swallowing properly), the

---

[28] An upper gastrointestinal endoscopy is a procedure that allows your doctor to look at the inside lining of your esophagus, your stomach and the first part of your small intestine.

food he would eat would come back up and a small portion of it could end up in his lungs creating congestion, hence leading to pneumonia. So, we go on with the newly prescribed medication and continue with his modified diet, in hopes that this would do the trick.

During the UGI, it was also found out that Rodney had what is called Gastroparesis or slow gastric emptying. So most of the foods that he took in, when they did go down the proper way, it took so much longer to travel down from his esophagus to his gut and then eventually be ready for voiding. It was noticed that the barium he had to swallow still had not moved through his body even after five hours. This presented another problem. So imagine if you have eaten a buffet, you are full, you relax and your food digests. Within a significant amount of time, you are hungry again because your food has been voided and your stomach is now empty. With Rodney, it would take a minimum of three to five hours for anything to begin to move, therefore creating a backup (so to speak) of his food.

In addition, to the upper portion of Rodney's body and the challenges he faced, there was an even more critical challenge that he faced every day of his life. If you recall, Rodney was born with hypotonic muscle (reduced or low) tone. One of the lasting challenges that he had to endure was that the low muscle tone was more damaging than anyone initially realized. With the food traveling slowly through his body, a lot of times it would sit. The low muscle tone would prohibit him from getting that feeling of needing to use the bathroom. Hence, it would not be until his bowel would become full to the brim that his body and brain would work hand in hand in telling him it was time to use the bathroom. However, by then, his waste had been sitting in his bowel for so long that it had stretched his bowel out of shape. I was once told by one of his gastroenterologists that in order to understand what Rodney's bowels were going through think of it as this. You have a balloon and you blow it up and put some water in it and tie it. You set in on a table for about a week and decide that you want to untie the balloon to pour the water out. Once the water has been poured out, the shape of the balloon remains as it was when it was filled up. It never regains its actual shape, so each time it is refilled and then emptied it never goes back to its normal state. This was again, due to his inability to bear weight down in order to void the waste from his body. After going on for so many years like this, his bowel would never go back to its original state.

The remedies for his bowel issues was of course more medication in addition to regular enemas. The medication that was prescribed to him was supposed to help retrain his bowel in addition to adding water to his bowels to make things easier. However, as Murphy's Law would have it with Rodney, this would only work temporarily.

I will never forget the first time I was sitting in the house Rodney and all of a sudden he begins to cough and choke. I jumped up and patted him on his back and raised his arms to help him to regain his composure. However, after turning him around to get a look at his face, I am faced with a surprisingly odd picture. I run to get some tissue to clean his face off. I look at it closely as I'm cleaning his mouth and his nose. I couldn't for the life of me figure out what this brown substance was that was coming from his mouth and nose. Initially, I thought maybe he had eaten some dirt while he had been playing out in the yard. After looking at the tissue closer, I realize that it wasn't dirt. Then I thought, well maybe it was the chocolate pudding from earlier. So I chalked it off as just that. He appeared to be fine and went on playing throughout the remainder of the day.

Later that night when he was sleeping, I heard him coughing and sounding as if he were going to choke again. I immediately ran into his room to see what was going on. As I turn the light on and head over to his bed, I notice that his face is covered again with that same brown substance and this time it's a great deal more and all over his pillow. I panic. Yet I spring right into action. I sit him up (actually I believe I snatched him up) so quick that I think I scared the poor child. I reach for the towel that I always keep by his bedside and start to clean him up. I know at this point that there is something seriously wrong. So I get him dressed, place his soiled t-shirt and his pillow case in a plastic bag and take him to the ER (yes the ER was my best friend and second home for years….thank God they are open 24 hours).

Once registered and settled in an examination room, we wait for a physician. The doctor comes in and asks what the problem is. I begin to tell him about the two events that occurred that day with Rodney, being as descriptive as possible. He looks at me bewildered as if I was crazy or possibly making things up. So, I pull the soiled items out of the bag and show it to him. I know that doctors see all types of different things in the ER, however, this particular doctor showed me in his facial expressions that he had never seen anything like this before. He recovered quickly and after he closed his mouth he cleared his throat and said, "Ms. Randolph, I believe at first glance and smell that this is feces. If it is, then we have a real serious problem on our hands." Feces (I asked in my head)? I looked at him and asked him out loud, "Did you say feces?" He nodded his head as he made his way over to the bed to examine Rodney's belly. He asked the normal questions about his diagnoses, eating habits, bowel habits, and medications. After pushing on his belly, attempting to look into his mouth with a tongue depressor (yeah that was a fight) and a rectal examination, he decided that an x-ray was in order to get a look at his belly and intestines.

As I sit watching Rodney sleep while we await the results of the x-ray, my thoughts become a little anxious. Thinking about the how serious this issue is. Wondering if it's something that is easily fixed. Just a bunch of thoughts swirling around in my head. Then I remembered that being anxious about finding things out that you have no control over just makes the problem seem bigger than it really is. What I did know was that no matter what was going on, that my being anxious was not going to fix or change it.[29] So I just decided to wait patiently and see what the end was going to be.

It wasn't too long after my little anxieties were calmed that the doctor walked in bringing along with him a second doctor. This second doctor introduced herself as a gastrointestinal physician. She asked me to give her an account of the events of earlier that day. I gave her all of the details and then showed her the soiled clothing. Then the doctors started to examine him again. One of them asked me when was Rodney's last bowel movement. I explained that it had been two or three days prior and that he didn't have them on a regular basis and never had in his entire life. The second doctor proceeded to tell me that they have looked at his x-ray and that Rodney's intestines were full to the brim. That was the reason he was choking. Even though he was hungry and eating, he had no more room for the food. Lord Jesus, help me!! I knew this was serious and possibly life

---

[29] "Cast all your anxiety on him because he cares for you." *1 Peter 5:7*

threatening. The gastro doctor continued on by saying they were going to admit him. They went on to explain that he was not going to be able to eat anything. They were going to bring in their pediatric specialist team to start him on some IV fluids to keep him from being dehydrated. The course of treatment, they explained, would be to receive a gallon at a time of Golytely (the liquid that is used for patients before a colonoscopy), to make him go to the bathroom. They expected it to be a pretty lengthy process because of the amount of stool that was inside of his intestines. Some of it, they figured, would be much harder to get out so they were going to reassess him after every gallon of the liquid suppository.

Since Rodney was not going to be able to take anything by mouth, I asked about his psychotropic medications. The doctors looked up the list of his current medications and stated that the doctors upstairs would be able to provide him with something comparable via his IV lines to keep him calm. After a few other questions back and forth, we were taken upstairs to a room.

This admission started off smooth (all things considered), until the first gallon of medication was administered. The medication was provided through his IV line and I really didn't know what to expect from it. However, it wasn't until after the first 12 hours and at the beginning of the second gallon of medication that there were any type of results. Just let me say that at that point, a nurse, a tech and myself had to pitch in to get him and his bed cleaned and changed. I know it sounds pretty disgusting and trust me it was. However, I would have never imagined that my son had that much waste in him.

At the end of the second gallon, an xray and examination was done again. Unfortunately, there was still some work to be done. So the gastro doctor ordered a third gallon of the Golytely. In the meantime, while losing all of this waste, Rodney was losing weight. He was beginning to look pretty puny and the poor baby couldn't do anything but lay there.

It was after the third gallon had been administered that Rodney was finally all cleaned out (and so was the daily laundry supply for that unit too, just kidding). The next step was to slowly start him on foods again and hopefully his body would be able to produce a bowel movement with just his regular constipation medication he took at home.

With an order for some applesauce and yogurt the first two days, everything appeared fine. The doctors were pleased with the progress he had made in transitioning to eating. They were also pleased with him being able to void what was being put in. Since the issue of severe constipation and impaction had been diagnosed, the doctor sent him home with an increased dosage of his daily medication.

Over the next month or so, things seemed to be continuing to work well. Rodney was eating food and he was still able to use the bathroom regularly. Well, his regular. He was still on most days not having a bowel movement, however, with the increased medication, I could generally get him to produce by day three.

Unfortunately, as time went on over the next year, there had been at least six more events of having severe constipation and impaction. It was then, that his current gastro doctor suggested that I try putting all of his food into a food processor. So, on the weekends, I would fix at least three different complete meals, put them into a food processor and store them for the week. These little containers became our best friends. It would appear that he was eating more at one point, and it became a concern because even when he was eating just the baby foods previously, he was still having the problems with constipation.

Over the next two years Rodney was in and out of the hospital because of his bowel issues. It appeared that no matter what we tried, what medications were added or changed, he was still unable to have regular bowel movements. There were instances of what the doctors believed there was an ileus[30]. With this type of dilemma, nothing is able to move through the intestines. Not solid foods, no liquids and not even gas. Nothing.

In a matter of three years, Rodney had a minimum of 10 hospital admissions inn both VA and NC and this issue was not getting any better. His gastro doctor during one of his many hospital admissions, suggested that they bring in a surgeon for a consult. This was not what I wanted to hear. However, I was sure that Rodney's body was tired from all the wear and tear of not working properly, the many IV lines to keep him hydrated and fed. I agreed to consult with the surgeon. The surgeon came into the hospital to assess Rodney's medical records including all of his hospitalizations for severe constipation, impactions, labs, x-rays and CT scans that surrounded these issues. After the assessment, the physician stated that Rodney was a candidate to be seen in the office and that the nursing staff

---

[30] An ileus is a blockage of the intestines caused by a lack of peristalsis. Peristalsis is the pumping action of the intestines that helps move from through the digestive system.

would coordinate the appointment with them and provide that information to me.

Rodney was discharged from the hospital on a Friday afternoon with an appointment at the surgeon's office on that Monday morning. Upon arrival to the appointment, I was nervous. I was unsure of what surgery could possibly be done to fix this issue. I sat with the surgeon and he explained to me that Rodney's digestive system (according to the x-rays and clinical notes he had seen), was in bad shape. He basically had very little motility through his digestive system and if it were not corrected, or another solution provided, it could end up disastrous in the long run. In addition to the lack of motility, his body was not receiving adequate nourishment through eating. The physician went on to explain to me about a procedure called a gastrostomy tube[31] (G-tube). He showed me via diagram where the G-tube would be placed and explained to me how the calculations for nourishment for Rodney's continued growth would be followed not only by him but also a nutritionist. The surgery itself would take less than an hour, with the hospital admission being no longer than two days. The hospital along with his office would coordinate all of the nutritional supplement supplies with a local company that would deliver the proper amount to us monthly.

Wow! This was a lot to take in at once. I had so many questions, the first was "so Rodney won't be able to eat by mouth any longer?" The doctor stated that it all depends on his desire to eat soft foods after the surgery. However, for the most part, he shouldn't be hungry because he will get

---

[31] A G-tube is a tube inserted through the abdomen that delivers nutrition directly to the stomach. It is one of the ways doctors can make sure kids with trouble eating get the fluid and calories they need to grow.

146

enough nutrition to fill him up daily. The next question was "Will he have to have the G-tube for the rest of his life?" The answer to that was "It all depends on how his body accepts it and his level of nutritional needs as he grows. However, with the chronic state of his digestive system, more than likely he will." I then asked, "Will he have to bedridden?" The doctor explained to me that no he would not have to be bedridden. The nutritionist would come up with a schedule for his feedings that would be conducive to his daily activities. The doctor went on to explain to me that the staff at the hospital and the supply company would provide me with all of the training that I would need to care for and possibly replace the Mic-key button[32]. The rest of the appointment was filled with another examination including measuring, labs and some refereeing between Rodney and the doctor because he wasn't up to having this new doctor touch, prod, poke in places that he didn't want to be touched. Before the appointment was over I had to stop back by the receptionist desk to sign a few more papers and to make sure all contact information was correct. This way the office would be able to contact me and let me know when the surgery was going to be scheduled. I was informed that if at all possible, it would be some time in the next week. The next week??!! Oh my. I truly wasn't expecting all of this to happen so quickly. Although this was not happening in my expected timeline (to this day I really don't think I had one, I was just nervous), I still accepted it and knew that this was going to be in my son's best interest.

The very next morning, I received a telephone call from the hospital's pre-op center. The nurse introduced herself and verified information about the surgery. She then went over

---

[32] A MIC-KEY button is inserted into your stomach through the abdominal wall. There is an inflatable balloon at one end and an external base at the other. This tube allows the intake of food and water that your body requires.

a very detailed list of questions to ensure that all of Rodney's up-to-date medical information was correct. At the end of our conversation, she stated that she would be calling me back before the end of the day with a date for admission.

As the nurse stated, she did call back and informed me that they were able to schedule Rodney for the surgery later that week. She provided me with further instructions as to where to check in upon arrival to the hospital and reminded me to bring his complete list of any prescriptions and over the counter medications he was currently taking. At the end of the conversation I was filled with two sets of emotions. Nervousness and relief. Needless to say, I was a little nervous because I had never imagined that this type of surgery would be playing a part in his health care needs. I had done some research since the appointment with the surgeon and I knew the statistics and they were pretty good as far as the success. The insertion of a g-tube was definitely where Rodney was in regard to his inability in receiving the needed nutrition for survival. I was relatively comfortable, but still nervous because as with any major surgery, there is always a tremendous risk. Then there was the relief in just knowing that this would be able to aid my son in not only his nutrition but to alleviate the uncomfortable pain which the doctor's assured me that he was having due to the constant emesis and severe constipation.

Over the next few days, I went on with our routine. One of the suggestions I was given was of course to elevate his head during sleep to minimize him choking in his sleep. I found this to help only a few times in the next few days. He still coughed and choked while sleep. It was just not as severe and it traveled down as opposed to pooling around his head and on his pillow while sleeping. This in itself was a big help. Unfortunately, It just was not the completion solution to his problem.

Thursday morning came and we arrived at the hospital and checked into through admissions as instructed. Once settled up in his room, I met with a number of doctors and nurses to go over the plan for the surgery and recovery time. I was told that the recovery time as an inpatient is generally two to three days and that everything had already been set up with the enteral supply company for all supplies needed and my training, which would take place there in the hospital.

Sleep for Rodney of course, was relatively easy. He was a little hyped because he had to have his meals withheld. This became an issue with him by late evening. However, I had already discussed this possibility with both doctors and nurses and all agreed that an extra sedative with his normal evening medications would be available if he became too aggressive. Fortunately, the extra dose of medication was just the ticket he needed and his night offered him a peaceful sleep. On the other hand, I was not able to get any sleep. I had expected it to be that way. However, by the time, I walked the halls a while, chatted with a few nurses and drank a cup of coffee, it was near time for him to go down to the surgical center.

I was allowed to go into the surgery suite where the actual procedure was going to take place. Again, more questions and answers. They allowed me to stand by his bed and talk to him while they were going through last minutes check offs. I did what I had done for several other occasions that presented themselves as scary to both Rodney and myself. I sang in his little ear. Our calming song for most difficult times was none other than Jesus Loves Me. As I sang softly to him I rubbed his little head. The staff worked around me and provided him with the anesthesia to put him to sleep. They told me at that point, I could leave and where to wait. Someone would come out and give me updates from time to time. I looked down again at Rodney aka Squirt and saw him sleeping peacefully. I kissed him on his forehead and said "see ya in a little while sweetie'" and then I left.

I knew that I was going to have a minimum of a 30-45 minute wait. Well at least that's the minimum time it takes for the surgery. I decided to go to the cafeteria and grab a bite to eat so I would not be sitting around waiting impatiently. In an attempt to time my return to the surgery waiting center and with the anticipated updated I expected, I rushed through my meal and made my way back to wait.

After waiting about 30 minutes, I started to get a little anxious. According to my estimated wait time, I should have received an update at least 15 minutes ago. So I decided to ask the receptionist if I had possibly missed someone from Rodney's surgical team and she stated that no one had come out as of yet. As I was returning to my seat, someone came to the waiting area and called my name. I turned and walked toward them. I was then informed that the surgery had taken a little longer than anticipated, however, they were wrapping things up and the doctor would be out to give me a recap of the procedure shortly. I asked why it had taken longer, but, all I could get was that she was unable to tell me and to just have a seat, it shouldn't be too much longer.

Now we all know in situations such as this. Our minds begin to race and think up the worse scenarios we can muster up. As my mind conjured up every possible thing that could go wrong I realized that I was allowing my thoughts to get the best of me. It was at that moment, I remembered one of the first scriptures ever memorized. In times of fear and anxiety[33], there was nothing else I could do but to go to that special place of calmness and I knew for a fact that God would meet me there.

As I sat in my chair with my eyes closed, I felt a sense of calmness coming over me. I started to take slow deep breaths and I could feel what would have been tension, slowly give way to a more relaxed feeling. After about a good five minutes or so, I heard my name being called again. I opened my eyes and the gastroenterologist was walking in my direction. I started to stand and she motioned me to stay where I was as she approached me. She sat next to me and began to inform me of the turn of events in the operating room. The beginning of the surgery went without any hitches at all. It wasn't until it was time to insert the MIC-KEY button that it was realized there were some issues with Rodney's intestines. There was an issue that was noticed as they were also doing another UGI examination. The doctor discovered that Rodney had a hiatal hernia.[34] The doctor went on to explain to me that it was more than likely the reason why his GERD was so severe. I asked the physician what was the cause of the hernia and she explained that it was due to his excessive coughing, retching, and lack of bowel movements. The GI doctor went on to explain because of the repair needed for the hernia as well as the insertion of the MIC-KEY button, the medical team made the decision to change his surgery from a laparoscopic surgery to an open surgery (an incision from below his chest to the top of his abdomen). After the surgeon was able to

---

[33] "I sought the Lord, and he answered me; he delivered me from all my fears." *Psalm 34:4 (NIV)*

[34] An internal body part that pushes into an area where it doesn't belong is called a hernia. The hiatus is an opening in the diaphragm – the muscular wall separating the chest cavity from the abdomen.

open his body up, it was realized that his GERD and the hiatal hernia had created so much damage that Rodney also needed a Nissen Fundoplication[35] - Nissen Wrap (which also keeps the acids and food from rising back up). The doctor explained also that this procedure (Nissen Wrap) usually lasts about 7-10 years. She went on to explain that once inside, the remainder of the surgery was a success and the feeding apparatus that remains in his stomach was in place and according to the x-ray done, was working as planned.

Whew!! Talk about a lot to take in. This was a great deal of information thrown at me yet again. I was ready to see my son. I needed to see him. I stood up and the doctor took my cue. As we were walking to the recovery room, she continued to explain that his initial 2-3 day stay would more than likely be extended to 5-7 days as a precaution to make sure he does not have any complications. I remember nodding my head and whispering" okay." Other than the normal questions I had about when the feeding process would begin, my only concern at the moment was to set eyes on Rodney.

As I entered the dimly lit room, the nurse turned from where she was at the head of his bed and smiled. She looked at me and said "Your handsome little boy is still sleeping and is doing fine." I tossed my belongings onto a chair in the corner of the room and walked over to where he was laying. I took notice of the various IV lines that were dripping. I

---

[35] During fundoplication surgery, the upper curve of the stomach (the fundus) is wrapped around the esophagus and sewn into place so that the lower portion of the esophagus passes through a small tunnel of stomach muscle. This surgery strengthens the valve between the esophagus and stomach (lower esophageal sphincter), which stops acid from backing up into the esophagus as easily. This allows the esophagus to heal.

looked up at the monitor that displayed his vital signs (something I had learned through the years). Everything looked good. There was a sheet over his legs just up to his hips. Eventually, my eyes landed on the reason we were here. There was a long and rather large strip of surgical tape midline his body. Underneath the tape I could see traces of blood. Approximately three inches from the bottom of the tape there was another section of tape that held what appeared to be an oversized pacifier with a long tube coming out of it. I leaned in closer and took a look at it. I asked the nurse, "Is this a different g-tube?" She went on to explain to me that this was a temporary one and that this one would be changed out for a more compact one in about 30 days. I asked the nurse, "So the feeds can be given through this one also?" She replied yes it could.

I continued to stand there quietly just watching my little boy sleep. He seemed so peaceful. After several minutes passed, the nurse instructed me to start talking to him in an attempt to wake him up. I started calling his name and messing with his fingers. The nurse and I took turns talking to him and calling out his name. He was really out of it. Not responding to anything. I messed with his ears, tickled him under his chin and played with his fingers some more. Finally, the nurse started to take the sheet off his feet and legs stating that it's possible that he is too comfortable and perhaps a little cool air will help to bring him around. Once his feet were exposed and with the two of us continuing to call his name, Rodney began to stir. His head began to move side to side ever so slightly. There was an unheard sigh of relief from both myself and the nurse. I started smiling and said, "I know you hear me little boy, so stop playing possum." I continued to talk to him and explained to him that I was right here with him and that everything was going to be alright. The nurse stepped out of the room for a few minutes. Upon her return, she informed me that she had checked the amount of anesthesia that had been given to him and found that he had received a sizeable dose and it could take a good amount of time before he was fully awake. She continued to tell me that the doctor said Rodney was fine to go upstairs to his room and that transport was waiting in the hall to take us back up.

Over the course of the day, Rodney slept mostly. He opened his eyes briefly several times but before I could get his attention he drifted off back to sleep. The nurse and the tech assigned to care for him continued to keep a close watch on him. Early evening, the unit's doctors came to make their rounds and were impressed with his surgical site. There was a discussion about the plan to continue to keep him sedated through the night to ensure that his movement was limited. I believe everyone was a little nervous about whether or not he would wake up and start pulling at the newly inserted apparatus or even pull at his incision. There was always a group effort in turning and rolling him to get his soiled diapers changed, being extra careful of his incision as well as his pain level.

His night went well and was a blessing to me because I was able to get some sleep. Well, as much as you can while you are in the hospital. Even though they were not coming in to see me, my eyes popped open every time the door opened.

Over the next twelve hours it was all about keeping him comfortable as he started to come out of his anesthetic induced slumber. It always took him an extra amount of time to reach his full out consciousness whenever he had been sedated. It had nothing to do with the anesthesia, it was just his genetic makeup. Once, he was fully awake, the doctors were able to better assess his level of pain and adjust his meds accordingly. By the evening after the surgery, it was decided they were going to start using his new g-tube. The plan was to start slowly with some Pedialyte at a very slow dose of only 5cc per hour (which is only a teaspoon per hour). If he tolerated it with no side effects, they would increase it by 5cc every six hours. The goal was to get him to tolerate a total of 85cc per hour before attempting to switch over to the enteral formula which he would be using at home to provide all of his nutrients and calories. All of his vitals were within the normal range, he seemed to be comfortable with the pain medication he was administered and after an examination it was noted that bowel sounds could be heard. He was moving along on the right track.

Throughout the night they were really closely monitoring him and the intake and output of fluids. By early the next afternoon his feedings had increased to 30cc per hour. I was coming in the room from getting some coffee and I stopped at his bed because the tech was standing beside him. I asked her if everything was alright. She said she wasn't sure which is why she was standing there. Rodney appeared to be sleeping. I called his name and did not get a response. I asked had he been back to sleep since I left the room (about 30 minutes prior) and she said he fell asleep about five minutes after I left. I called his name again and leaned closer in to him. As I leaned in I saw what I thought was him beginning to move. The movement stopped abruptly. Something inside of me told me to not move and to continue to watch him. A few seconds later, the movement started again in his legs. It was a rhythmic movement in both of his legs. I tapped him on his shoulder as I said his name yet again. No response. I moved my focus to his legs. They were shaking again. I looked at the tech and told her to go get the nurse and to tell her I believe that Rodney was having a seizure. In the meantime, his legs stopped moving. I continued to try and wake him by calling his name repeatedly. At that time the nurse comes into the room with the tech asking me what's going on. I gave her a description of what the tech and I had just seen prior to her joining us. She asked me if Rodney had a history of seizures. I stated that he did not. She looked him over and attempted to make an assessment that she doubted it were seizures and it was more than likely a side effect of him coming off the anesthesia. At that very moment, the rhythmic tremor started again in his legs. The nurse reached over and put her hand on one of his legs firmly. She stated, "If it's a seizure and you place firm pressure on the limb, the shaking won't stop." The shaking did not stop. She looked at her watch and continued to watch him. The tremors stopped after 30 seconds. Immediately after his legs stopped shaking, (about 10 seconds), they began again and this time his shoulders could be seen moving in the same rhythm as his legs. She looked at me as she picked up her phone and said, "Yes, he is seizing." She placed a call to the doctor and explained to him what she was witnessing. As she hung up the phone, the seizure stopped and she began to look into his eyes and look at the monitor to check his vitals since he was still hooked up to monitor his blood pressure, oxygen and heart rate. At this time, the doctor along with a few students, rushed into the room. Everyone made a space for themselves around the bed in order to get a good view of him. Unfortunately, they did not have to wait too long to see what the nurse (and myself after they asked questions) explained to them what we had seen. The doctor examined him and decided to wait it out for a few minutes because it could be as the nurse stated just his body reacting to coming off the anesthesia. If it continued or worsened, they would start him on a dose of seizure medication. We, the tech and myself, (there has always been a tech in the room with me to assist me around the clock), should call the nurse when and if we were to see these movements again.

So the two of us pulled our chairs close to his bed in order to keep a close watch on him. An hour or so had passed and we had not seen any further seizure activity. It came time for the tech to leave and her replacement came into the room. As the tech was briefing her replacement on what was going on, Rodney started seizing again. Before I could say anything or even reach for the call bell to signal the nurse, the small rhythmic tremors that we witnessed earlier became a more forceful shake. He was in fact having a full blown seizure. We pressed the call bell and the relief tech ran out to the hall and yelled for a nurse at the same time. Before I knew it, the room was full of medical staff. I stepped out of the way so they could get close to him. It looked like total chaos. I could hear one of the nurses on the phone with what I found later to be the pharmacy asking for some STAT seizure medication. One of the doctor's (who had ran out of the room), came back in with a package. As he was tearing it open several of the nurses positioned themselves on either side of the bed and gently rolled him to his side (in an effort to not damage his incision) while another bared his bottom in preparation for what the doctor was taking out of the package. The doctor positioned himself closer to the bed and lowered the bedrails and quickly administered what I thought was an enema and later found out that it was an emergent suppository for seizures. I don't think anyone had noticed that I had begun to lean on the wall and then eventually made my way to my chair and then just plopped down. I was devastated. I was at a total loss for words. I could say nothing but, "Oh God, please help him." I knew that in this trying time with my heavy heart, there was nothing that I could do to help my child. I felt helpless. Then I remembered (and God has a way of bringing you back to your center), that if I had not learned anything through these years of raising my boys, I learned to stand on His holy word. His promises. I knew that in Him I could find the strength that I needed to commandeer my way through this storm.[36] I quickly said, "Thank you Jesus." I knew that by giving Him thanks in advance, that no matter how bleak any situation we are faced with, that giving Him the praise and believing that we will come out victorious is enough to give me the strength to carry on. As I mustered up the strength to stand back up, I noticed that Rodney's seizure had stopped.

I walked back over to the bed and my eyes met with the doctor's. He looked at me as if to say he understood the dismay that my face must have been showing. He motioned for me to come to the other side of the room away from where the nurses were still standing and working and getting Rodney resituated in his bed. He explained to me that at least one-third of children with the ATR-X syndrome have seizures at some point. He went on to say that he was relieved that we were able to spot it at the onset. He had also decided after witnessing these seizures that he wanted to start him on a regimen of seizure medications through his IV line. He would also, he continued, set up to have an EEG done on him as soon as possible. The medication he had given him was just an emergency medication and that he had already called down to the pharmacy to have an ongoing dose of another seizure medication administered. He asked me to ensure that if I see any other seizure activity to do as we had just done and notify his nurse. I asked him if the seizures were to be ongoing and he said he really could not be sure. However, they would continue to keep a close watch on him. The staff started to leave and ensured me one by one that everyone would be assisting in keeping him as safe and comfortable as possible.

---

[36] "My soul is weary with sorrow; strengthen me according to your word." *Psalm 119:28 (NIV)*

Throughout the night, Rodney had several more seizures lasting between 30 and 90 seconds each. With each incident, the staff did just as they stated by coming and ensuring that all was well with not just him but me. By the morning, the doctors were called back in because it was evident that the medication he was receiving was not strong enough to hold his seizures off. The staff was pretty much scratching their heads at the medication vs this little boy. They just didn't have an understanding of how this little boy who was medically fragile and barely weighed 75 pounds was resistant to some of the strongest seizure medications they were able to prescribe for a child. So by mid-morning, the doctors called in his neurologist and had him consult with them and decided to add a second seizure medication to run piggyback with the first one.

The morning proceeded and I cat napped in the chair. Once I was up from my little nap, I decided to go over and attempt to wake Rodney up. When I looked at him, he looked flushed, so I decided to feel his forehead. It was hot. I asked the tech if she would take his temperature. It was 105.7. I knew what that meant automatically. Rodney had more than likely contracted something since his surgery. We called the nurse who in turn called the doctor. Medications were provided to bring his fever down and some blood was drawn and sent to the lab.

While we were waiting for the lab results to come back, the doctor ordered a few other tests. Upon his examination of Rodney, he was listening to his breathing, which had become a little rapid, the doctor also noticed a rattling in his chest. No sooner than he heard the rattling, Rodney began coughing which made the ratting more apparent. The doctor ordered an x-ray to be done immediately. His breathing was a tad bit faster, along with the fever and the rattling in his chest, pointed toward one thing....pneumonia, the doctor stated. He did not want to say absolutely 100% until the labs had returned and the x-ray had been done. However, he was almost certain that this was what was going on with Rodney. Taking into consideration of Rodney's inability to move around after his surgery, the changes in his body because of the surgery and his history of pneumonia, the doctor said he felt comfortable with treating him as such until the results were back. So he ordered a bolus of a very strong antibiotic to get him started. Continuing to examine him, he also noticed that there was some type of fluid seeping from underneath the bandage over Rodney's incision. He requested the nurse to bring in some sterile materials and swabbed the fluid then sent it down to the lab also. In the interim, the doctor had the surgeon paged to examine him.

A couple of hours pass and all the labs come back and the x-ray was done, everything was positive for pneumonia. The surgeon had come and determined that the seepage was nothing to be too alarmed about and had instructed on a daily dressing change and to closely monitor it. However, while waiting for all of the results to come back, Rodney's condition changed drastically. His temperature refused to go down and stay down. His cough became hard and persistent. They immediately began talks of transferring him to the ICU. The surgeon and doctor both agreed that he could provide more intense care and monitoring there. They also agreed to stop his feedings into his g-tube at the time because of the seepage until they could get him back on the right track.

I was disappointed but yet I truly supported both doctors' recommendations. I knew that it didn't take long for Rodney to get sick. The slightest change in him generally allowed for an attack of anything that can bring his health down. I knew intense treatment was what he would need not only now but definitely over the next few days. As the process started of switching him over, I began to notice his breathing was getting worse. I informed the nurse and she said they (the medical staff) had already discussed it outside of the room and the doctor had already ordered for him to be on oxygen to support him.

Shortly after all of these events occurred, Rodney was taken to ICU. Breathing faster, heart rate elevated, temperature still up, on oxygen and not able to wake up. Sounds pretty harrowing. Well it was. This time, there were not as many questions to answer because most information was passed on by his previous attending staff. Once situated, I sat down beside him and realized how different he was beginning to look. His color had changed and become pale. He looked sickly. Weak. However, I knew I couldn't dwell on how he looked. I needed to focus on the big picture and that was knowing in my heart that yes he may have a long, bumpy road to his baseline of health, but I needed to focus on knowing that he would get there.

During his time in the ICU, he was faced with many battles. There were days that he appeared to be getting better, all for things to turn around and prove him to be worse the next day. It was what you would call a roller coaster ride. After being in the ICU for three weeks and having many high strength doses of antibiotics, amount of oxygen levels change, bags on top of bags of IV fluids, and countless blood draws, x-rays and without a doubt prayers, Rodney was being transferred back to the main pediatric unit.

Back to square one with his new feeding tube, he was immediately started on Pedialyte again. With the same schedule of starting with 5cc per hour and titrating up to 85cc per hour, we were all hoping for the best. Over the next 24 hours all of the nurses that had been assigned to him previously would peep in his room just to see how he was doing. All hoping for the best and wishing him well. Blowing him kisses and even some coming in to his room to tickle him or give out hugs. As a little boy, who loves being the center of attention, this was probably one of the best therapies he could have been given. The enteral feedings from the Pedialyte was working. He was perking up, his bowels were moving and he was starting to sit up more. It was time. The next step was to slowly move him from the Pedialyte to the enteral formula he would be getting all of his nutrition from. After meeting with the nutritionist again and going over the calculations needed to provide him with the proper amount of nutrition, we received the green light. His doctor made the determination when to start the enteral formula that day and how often the rate per hour would be titrated and the goal rate to achieve.

Three days later, there is a visit from a team of doctors that have arrived in Rodney's room that morning. Everyone is chipper and smiling. Each one of them took their time examining Rodney, listening to his breathing and talking to him. Each one of the team members provided me with their update on Rodney's progress and their overall prognosis. I was informed that since he had been in the hospital over a month and had missed his appointment in the doctor's office to change from the temporary feeding tube to the MIC-KEY button, that they would be able to change it out today. They also informed me that staff from the supply company would be in later that day to provide training to me about the care and replacement of everything. With all of this new information they were providing me, led me to ask one question. "Is he going home soon?" The lead doctor looked at me and said, "Yes. The plan is to discharge him tomorrow." Thank you Jesus. The day I had been waiting for was finally here. I was relieved and I'm sure Rodney would be even more relieved to go home, sleep in his bed and see his brother.

Rodney was discharged and we made it home. He was still a little weak. However, he definitely had his voice back and was yelling and screaming. I set him up in the living room to keep him from having the desire to walk down stairs. So he, Rodell and I made the living room into our bedroom over the next week. I was very nervous at first. All I could think about was what if, and how I would be able to handle it if the button came out of his stomach.[37] With each passing day, I became more confident in feeding him through his tube. Rodney's strength returned and he was back on his feet before I knew it. The one thing about him was when he got sick, he really got sick. However, he had the strength of a true warrior and would ultimately fight his way back.

Over the next year Rodney was faced with minimal changes to his medical condition. His seizures were being controlled by several medications. The enteral feedings were going well. He was tolerating it and had picked up a few pounds. He continued to have issues with severe constipation and had been admitted in the hospital several times for complete cleaning and treatment. Then one day, his belly started to swell. I noticed it as I was preparing him for school. I made a mental note to give him some extra medication that afternoon when he returned home.

---

[37] So do not fear, for I am with you; do not be dismayed, for I am your God. I will strengthen you and help you; I will uphold you with my righteous right hand. *Isaiah 41:10 (NIV)*

When Rodney came home from school, his whole demeanor was different from when I saw him that morning. He was a little sluggish and once I was able to get him into the house he just plopped down on the couch and fell back. That was totally off his routine of going through the cabinets in the kitchen and screaming at the top of his lungs. I laid him down and felt his head, no fever. I lifted his shirt and watched his chest for his breathing pattern. He appeared to be taking shorter breaths. I felt his belly and it was definitely distended and very firm. I decided to take him off his enteral feeds and allow him to rest a while. As he drifted off to sleep, I retrieved the medication for his constipation, pulled it up in a syringe and pushed it through the tube into the MIC-KEY button. This medication may take a while to work so after 30 minutes, I removed the tube from the MIC-KEY button and keeping the flap to the button open allowed it to vent in an attempt to let any gas that was in his stomach seep out. Normally, when this was done, the gas would start escaping immediately. I left him there sleeping for about an hour and when I returned, his stomach was harder than when I had given him the medications and opened the port to vent. I didn't become worried at that point, because there had already been several occasions over the last year when this scenario had played itself out. So I knew the next step was for me to give him another dose of the medication through his tube.

Over the next few hours, nothing seemed to make any progress with Rodney's bowels or the swelling in his stomach. He was still sleeping on the couch. I decided to get him up to his room and continue to work with a few options I had to see if I would be able to get him to use the bathroom.

Throughout the night I continued to check for any differences in his stomach. There was no progress at all. I had gone through all of my options and he still had not used the bathroom. I decided at the break of dawn that I would contact his physician once the office opened.

That morning, I contacted his physician in an attempt to get an appointment in the office. Instead of having me bring Rodney into the office, I was instructed to take him to the ER to get an x-ray and have them contact his office after it was done.

Getting Rodney to the hospital when he was sleeping and not able to stay away for more than a few seconds at a time was a task in itself. However, I made it there with him. Providing all medical personnel with a background of what had been going on and what Rodney's physician had instructed me to have done, we were led to the back.

Through all of the moving and undressing and prepping him for the x-ray, Rodney pretty much stayed sleep. He was in and out of sleep but only keeping his eyes open still for only a few seconds at a time. When he was awake he was pretty lethargic, so the IVs were inserted and started to keep him hydrated. Once the x-ray was done, an ER physician came in and stated he had received the x-ray results, sent the images to Rodney's doctor and consulted with him. Rodney would be admitted into the hospital. It appeared that not only was he full again of feces, but it was believed that there may be a section of his intestines that had an obstruction or may even be twisted.

Over the course of the day, it was pretty much the same routine as most of his admitting diagnosis had not changed from his previous stay. However, due to the possibility of his intestines being twisted a CT scan was ordered in to get a better view of what was going on. Through most of this time, Squirt drifted in and out of sleep. Once the CT scan was done and read, it was diagnosed that he did in fact have a portion of his intestines that was twisted. The only way to remedy it with him was to take him back into surgery. Again, late at night, Squirt was prepped for surgery, which was supposed to last approximately an hour.

Waiting for another surgery was no less anxious than the last wait for me. I gathered my thoughts as I settled into a chair with my coffee in the waiting room. I chatted with a friend and waited that hour. It was approximately 1-1/2 hours into the waiting that I decided to find someone who could check in and give me an update. I was getting a little worried at that point and needed to hear that everything was okay. Finally about 15 minutes later, the surgeon came out to speak with me. She explained to me that some complications had come up during the surgery. Rodney's intestines were in fact, twisted pretty badly. On top of that he had a great deal of scar tissue around his intestines and underneath the incision from his previous surgery. There was so much scar tissue that she was unable to determine how and where to detach it without damaging his intestines further. She continued to explain to me that there was an option that would omit using the g-tube to feed him. It was called a j-tube. The difference between the both is that the MIC-KEY button is placed on the opposite of his abdomen so that all feeds go straight to his intestines as opposed to his stomach as in the g-tube. Also in addition to all of the scar tissue, his reflux had continued to burn and damage his esophagus. His reflux had progressed so much that because of his retching his stomach had gone up through his diaphragm and was cemented to the back of his chest. She would be able to separate it but would need to make a second incision and go through his thoracic cavity.[38] In addition, the Nissen Wrap which had also been done when the g-tube was placed (approximately 18 months prior) had come undone (normally they last 7-10 years). The g-tube would remain in place and would more than likely be able to be used to administer his medications while the j-tube would be specifically used for feeding him. The surgeon asked me if I were okay with the insertion of the j-tube and the repair of the Nissen Wrap. I agreed to both parts of this surgery. I was informed at that time, that the surgery should be another few more hours. The surgeon suggested that my friend and I go and have some coffee and a bite to eat in order to try and relax a bit. We agreed and the doctor quickly entered back into the operating suite.

Over the next few hours, there was an array of emotions from both my friend and I. We chatted, about all that Rodney had been through. I shared the story about how when he was born and all of the medical issues he had faced from the start. I also explained how within the first year of his life, how a physician had told me that he more than likely would not make it to see the age of eleven. I went on to talk about the many hospitalizations (even those that I just don't have the time to touch on in this book). The obstacles he had overcome to this point of not being able to walk until he turned three, talking at first then regressing when he reached the age of 2-1/2, and the list went on and on. It was well after midnight when the surgery was finally over. We went in to see Rodney and found him bundled up, with pillows all around him and still under the anesthesia. The nurse was just finishing up with cleaning him off, she said and was

---

[38] The thoracic cavity (chest cavity) is the chamber of the human body that is protected by the thoracic wall (rib cage and associated skin. The thoracic cavity also includes the cardiovascular system. (Wikipedia)

going to be adding an additional bag of medications and administering more pain medications as soon as the pharmacy dropped them off. I sat down beside him and let out a huge sigh of relief. Just because of me being able to set eyes on him, I knew that God did it again!! Even with all of the machines doing what they do and the lines going into veins pushing some form of medication into his body, I counted this as a victorious surgery. I was so thankful to see that everything appeared to be alright and even more grateful that I have an ongoing prayer life with my Savior Jesus Christ.[39]

Over the next week, everything with Rodney was on track with his healing process in the ICU. There of course, was another bout of seizures that he had to endure. Some were pretty bad and required a lot of medical attention, while others were able to be stopped immediately with a small increase of seizure medication. Once Rodney started showing signs of being able to sit up and became vocal he was transferred to the regular medical unit. The first two days was full of lots of loud noises, screams, laughter and shaking of the bed rails to get the attention of his nurse. By day three of him being out of ICU, I started to see a change in his energy level. He was starting to become less energized as the days went by. I bought this to the attention of his nurse. She stated to me that it was just because he had just had major surgery and been in ICU and she brushed me off. That did not set well with me of course, but I made a mental note to continue to keep a close eye on him. The next day Rodney had no interest in watching TV, listening to his music or even sitting up to play. Again, that mother's instinct kicked in telling me to speak up and say something to someone. I contacted the nurse for that night and explained the same thing I had to the nurse from the previous

---

[39] "Therefore I tell you, whatever you ask for in prayer, believe that you have received it, and it will be yours." *Mark 11:24 (NIV)*

day. My friend and I explained in detail what we had seen the last few days since Rodney had been out of ICU. This nurse, thought it was kind of strange also, especially since the two days prior when she was caring for him, he was full of energy. She agreed that we should keep a close watch on him through the night. I eventually left that night while Rodney was sleeping in order to prepare for Rodell's birthday the next day.

I decided that since I had been spending so much time at the hospital of late with Squirt, that I would take Roc out for breakfast to get his favorite pancakes before taking him to school. As we were pulling up into the parking lot to the restaurant, my cell phone rang. I grabbed soon as I recognized the hospital phone number. I could hear a bunch of noise in the background as the individual on the other side of the phone informed me that he was head of the pediatric ICU and that he had been called over to the regular pediatric unit because my son was having some difficulties. He went on to inform me that he had me on the speaker phone and a nurse was there that could witness our conversation. The intensivist explained that Rodney had a very low fever, an increased heart rate and his blood pressure was extremely low. He had also had an emergency x-ray done only to find out that Rodney's intestines appeared to be failing. Bottom line my son had become a victim of sepsis.[40] The doctor went on to tell me that they were currently preparing Rodney to go to emergency surgery to go back into his incision to look at his intestines as soon as they were able to get into the emergency room. Oh my God!! I was livid. Yes livid. Not because this was happening, but because I kept telling the nurse the night before that there was something wrong with my child; yet no one would listen. The intensivist asked how long before I could get there (by then we were already

---

[40] Sepsis – a whole-body inflammation caused by an infection.

backing out of the parking lot to take Roc to school) and I said, soon as I drop Roc off, I'm on my way. I hung up after they told me where to come upon my arrival.

I ran into the school practically dragging Rodell in with me. Fortunately, I did not have to wait, I was able to brief the front office on what was going on and to let his teacher know that I will call later to make arrangements for someone else to pick him up if necessary. I immediately left and we were able to get to the hospital in record time (thanks to my forever friend who was my driving my van like it was a NASCAR race).

As we arrived, I was able to catch up with the medical staff as they were going through the last hallway before taking Squirt into surgery. I had just enough time to run up behind them and ask them to stop and give him a quick kiss and tell him that I loved him. It was at that point that I felt dizzy and dry mouth. I knew I needed to sit down. I did but just for a few minutes. Once my head was together, I looked for the first person back up on the regular floor that could tell me anything about the morning's events concerning Rodney. The only information I received was pretty much the same information that I had given them the last two days. Rodney had been showing signs of not feeling well, even though they had been telling me it was just because he was post op and would be alright. His body temperature had dropped that morning along with his blood pressure. Thanks be to God that the nurse who had him under her care that morning, had also had him the previous day and knew that I had concerns about his regressing. She immediately called in the attending doctor who in turn had the intensivist paged to come and take a look at Rodney. This was one of those moments in life that you are generally upset because no one wanted to listen yet thankful that someone did. Finally.

With this information provided, we went back down to the waiting room for Rodney to come out of surgery. Again.

Now I have never been through as many surgeries as Squirt has. However, I can only imagine after being out of surgery for only a little over one week and then being faced with having to go back into surgery through the same incision had to be really tough on his little body. I still trusted and believed in God's intervention on all of this. His hand was already in it by allowing the same nurse to be present and attentive when I wasn't there. Things such as this are the reasons why I never liked leaving my sons at the hospital, even though I may have to stay there weeks at a time. So to God be the glory for his covering.

Several hours passed and finally the intensive care doctor came out to let me know that all was well. He was so happy that he had been able to get Squirt to the operating table when he did because he found that his intestines had a kink in them from his previous surgery and it would have been fatal had it not been caught in time. He told me that he would have him placed back in the ICU so they could ensure that he received an ample amount of antibiotics to clear his blood stream of any infection from the sepsis and to be able to monitor him even more closely. He took me back to where Rodney was resting peacefully and heavily medicated.

My baby boy looked tired. Even in his sleep. What I saw was a little boy who had been through so much and I felt as though I wanted to just climb in the bed with him and hold him close and never let him go. However, I knew that would not be possible because in due time, he would be back to normal and pushing his mama away from him so he can be mischievous.[41] I grabbed his hand and leaned over to kiss his cheek and said, "Hey there Champ.....good to see you." The nurse filled me in on most of the same information that the doctor had already given me. After about an hour passed, Rodney still had not opened his eyes and the staff figured he would not because he was under anesthesia for so long. His vitals were good and the incision had minimal bleeding, so he was transported up to ICU so they could settle him into his room.

Since this was a re-opening at the same surgical site as well as having to fight off the sepsis, Rodney stayed in the ICU, for about a three weeks before he was transferred back out to the regular floor. There was a joyous reception once we arrived on the floor, with everyone shouting and smiling for his return. All of the nurses took their time to say 'welcome back' or 'glad to see you buddy' and even a 'miss you Squirt'. The medical staff who had over the years had become an extended family to us, were so relieved that all had ended well with his last emergency.

Over the next few weeks, the same routine of starting his enteral feeds through his j-tube were followed in the same manner as with his g-tube. Medications for his constipation was the only medication administered through the j-tube and in an aggressive manner, while all other meds were administered through his g-tube. From Pedialyte to the enteral feeds to psychotropic medications, and physical therapy because he had been bedridden just about a total of six weeks from the initial admission (the end of September), to making it to discharge day. It was a rough road but my

---

[41] As it is written: "I have made you a father of many nations." He is our father in the sight of God, in whom he believed – the God who gives life to the dead and calls into being things that were not. *Romans 4:17 (NIV)*

warrior pushed through it all. He was discharged and I happily took him home right before Christmas (December 2009).

Moving along over the next few years, there were no other major issues with Rodney. I found out after trying so many over the counter and prescription medications, that no matter what was added to his daily regimen, Squirt was still going to have issues with his bowels. It was just going to be something that he and I would have to constantly work on.

From January 2012 until May 2013, Rodney had a couple of short hospital stays surrounding his bowel issues (when they could not be resolved at home) along with one or two instances when he had pneumonia. During those illnesses, of course his seizures would kick in and medications would have to be tweaked in order to stop them. Overall, this timeframe was a year when he was the least sick since he had taken his first breath.

As you all know, my youngest son made his transition to life everlasting in May 2013. Everyone has always asked me how I was able to move on and not fall apart. Well you know when someone tells you "God will only put on you what you can bear?" This was His covering for me at that time. Having to deal with the passing of my son in May 2013 (my mom in June 2013, my dad in July 2013, and my grandfather in January 2014), I had a lot on my plate as far as dealing with emotions. I thank God even to this day how much He loved me to give me that cushion of not having to deal with Rodney's illness for a year in order to allow me to grieve and mourn my family members.

It was May 2014, exactly one year after Roc had passed, that things changed. Rodney wakes up and his stomach is super distended and was hard as a brick. Larger than it has ever been. It was so swollen that he couldn't even sit up. He was having trouble breathing and he was sweating. When I attempted to sit him up, his breaths became labored. I elevated his head on a few pillows in order to make him comfortable. I disconnected him from his feeding tube and began working on giving his medications in an attempt to get his bowels moving. Enema, Miralax, laxative and flushed with lots of water. A few hours went by and he was still having the same issues. I knew at that time because nothing had passed through his intestines, he was going to need a more aggressive treatment than what I was able to do for him. There was no need for me to contact his pediatrician, I already knew what she was going to say; take him to the ER. So I gathered him up and set out to the hospital.

Once arriving to the hospital, there was no change in him so he was rushed to the back immediately. Upon his assessment and the normal x-ray, Rodney was diagnosed with 'intestinal pseudo-obstruction'[42]. The doctor explained to me that not only was he severely constipated again, but that the x-ray showed a good deal of air in his intestines. The air in the intestines could come from his sleeping with his mouth open or the way he gulps to swallow. With his intestines lacking the peristalsis needed to move food through them, the only thing they would be able to do for him would be to take him off his feeds, hydrate him and provide him with an aggressive laxative regimen. He was admitted into the hospital where he spent the next week being treated. Upon discharge, Rodney aka SugaPimp (a

---

[42] A clinical syndrome caused by severe impairment in the ability of the intestines to push food through. Clinical features can include abdominal pain, nausea, severe distension, vomiting, diarrhea and constipation.

nickname that was given to him by a close family friend), was back to his baseline and filled with joy and laughter.

He returned to school and was moving along through the month until right before the end of the school year, and unfortunately, he awoke with the same exact scenario as he had a couple of weeks prior. Due to the amount of constipation medications and how any of his illnesses affected, they always led to an increase in his seizures, I had to return to the ER with him again.

Upon this admission, the doctors had become so familiar with him that there was no trial and error in his treatment. At this point, they were already aware of what worked, what did not and did not waste any time getting him started with his treatment. Again, the seizures, came and gave us all a big scare. However, just as quickly as he was admitted and they started, the staff was able to stop the seizures, follow his intestinal treatment and have him discharge in yet again another week.

The summer of 2014, proved to be no match for SugaPimp. When he was having a good day, he would yell and scream out, bang on the front door of the house, and turn the knob in an effort to get outside and walk up and down the sidewalk. As much as the heat would get to me in the middle of the day, Rodney's desire to be outside was equivalent to it. So he would attend summer school and then no later than 12 or 1, he would be begging to go outside in the heat. I could not be upset or tell him I didn't want to go in the heat. Who I was I to tell this young man, now 17 years old (6 years past what the doctors said he would live) and had fought through so much that I couldn't take the heat? So you know it, out in the hot sun, we went. In the evenings, he would always want to go for a ride. This was something I used to do when the boys were younger and fighting. I would put the both of them in the back of my vehicle and just ride to calm them down. So, when he wanted to go for a ride and we were already outside, he knew to walk to our vehicle and bang on either the back door or window to let me know he was ready to go. So we rode. No real destination. Just a ride anywhere was good enough for him.

For the remainder of the summer, Rodney was not able to attend summer school. Due to another bout with fighting his constipation and seizures that landed him in the hospital, he missed the remainder of the summer school year. By the time the 2014-2015 school year rolled around, he (as well as I), were ready for him to go back to school. The look of joy on his face once he was dressed early in the morning and outside waiting for his bus was always priceless. He would stand on one end or the other of the wheelchair ramp and glance back and forth looking for his bus. Especially paying attention to any type of vehicle that sounded like a school bus, be it trash truck or a metro bus, he watched it until he realized it was not his bus.

With school in session, I had become a tad nervous. To see Rodney smiling daily even though he was in a fragile medical state, I made sure that I was on top of my A-game more so than ever in ensuring all of his medical needs were met. I knew from experience that the slightest bug going around, he was susceptible to catching it. This in turn, would weaken his immune system and open the door for his already reoccurring medical problems. It was in October that he came down with a pretty nasty cold. For most people, that can be a relatively easy fix. However, with him, as noted before, it can turn his life upside down. As his symptoms kicked in, my adrenalin did also. For the next week, I kept

176

him home because he was having a difficult time. However, all thanks to God, my SugaPimp did not end up at the hospital. Whoopee a victory again!

We have entered into the month of November 2015 and it starts off with a bang. The constipation is back. I increase his meds and keep him home from school. Nothing worked. On this particular day, I noticed as the day went on, his stomach was becoming a bit more distended. His energy level was decreasing so he walked himself into his room and laid down on his own. After a while I went in to check in on him and he was sweating profusely and his stomach had become even more distended. It was so swollen that again he could not sit up and his skin was shiny because it was so stretched. His heart was beating so hard that I could see the rhythm in his neck from the bottom of his bed. I knew he was very uncomfortable and that everything I had tried to use to work on him earlier was not going to help. This incident was a little different. He seemed to be more uncomfortable. He was just really out of it and appeared to be getting worse by the minute. So my friend and I dress him and off to the ER we go again.

By the time, he had been through triage and was settled in a room in the ER, the doctor came in and looked him over and said, "Okay let's do another x-ray and see what he is looking like tonight."

The x-ray is done and upon his return, the nurse places the IV in his arm to prepare for fluids that we already know he will need. When the doctor returns, with what I believed was going to be a consult informing me that he will be admitted so they can clean him out, turns out to be something I truly did not expect. The physician looks at me and says, "Rodney is in bad shape. I have already contacted the surgeon…." I looked at him closer with my eyes squinted and say "Surgeon? What are you talking about?" The ER physician informs me that what he and the x-ray technician as well as the head of radiology saw in the x-rays does not look good. They each stated that they had never seen anyone's bowels look the way that Rodney's looked. Even with all of his previous incidences with this issue, they had never seen it this bad and they took it upon themselves to contact the surgeon, send the films to him over the computer because he was at home and he was on his way.

My head was spinning. I looked over at my friend who said, "Let's just wait to see what the surgeon has to say when he gets here." No sooner than that was said the surgeon rushes into Rodney's ER room. It is someone who is familiar with Rodney and has treated and co-treated him several times before. When he saw my face he immediately says, "Ms. Randolph, our boy isn't doing well. I know that we have talked since his last surgery and all have been in agreement that we didn't feel comfortable in allowing him to have any more surgeries." I responded with, "Yes. You are absolutely right. I don't want to get to the position where we are playing God with him." The surgeon nodded his head and looked at me solemnly as he said, "I have never been so much in agreement with anyone. He has been through a great deal. However, with all that I see with his intestines, the pseudo-obstruction and all of his other symptoms, if I do not operate on his tonight, he may not make it out of the ER. This is the reason why I rushed from home to here because I know what type of mother you are and I know you have always wanted the best for him. I support you in whatever decision you make. If you decide to go through with it, then the operating room is already booked because I took care of it before I left to come here."

If I had not been there every step of the way for the last 17 years in all of his medical issues, I may not believe what the doctor was saying to me. However, having a front row seat and being a key player in not only his development but all of Rodney's medical challenges, I knew what the doctor had just said was true. I knew in my heart at that very moment just by looking at my handsome son, that if something wasn't done to help him, then he would not make it out of the ER.

The doctor excused himself from the room as he said he would allow me a few minutes to discuss this over with my friend. Looking to someone else for answers or advice is one of the hardest things you can do when it is concerning your child. Have you ever been in a situation that you needed to make a decision and it was one of those decisions you wished that someone else could make for you? This was one of those. I didn't want to put my child through anything else unnecessary. However, if I did not make the decision to do the surgery, I felt as if I were just giving up on him. We talked a little bit more about his previous surgeries and how he overcame all of the challenges he had faced with them. I acknowledged how much strength he had for such a young man. I also acknowledged the fact that I believe he had to be getting tired because his little body had been through so much. I knew that with any type of surgery that there were no guarantees. I knew that even without all of medical issues that Rodney had, if this had been an atypical person going in for any other medical procedure, there still are no guarantees.

Within five minutes, the surgeon returned to the ER room asking whether or not I had made any type of decision. I looked over at my friend, took a deep breath, looked at the surgeon, and gave my permission for the surgery. He went on to explain to me that the he would be going into the same incision in order to get to his intestines again. With all of the problems that he had previously, he would most definitely be in the ICU and more than likely start him on heavy antibiotics, oxygen (because Rodney is one of those patients that forgets to breathe when he should be coming out of sedation), all of the monitors would chart his vitals of course and they would also have him hooked up to several ongoing fluids for hydration and pain. I am sure at this point I could have probably told the doctor what medications he should or would be prescribing for Rodney. I said a quick prayer as I watched the nurses and transport personnel prepare to take him to the operating room.

When we arrived to the surgical waiting room, there was not a soul there. It was late, approximately 9:00 p.m. so it was after normal business hours. We found a couple of chairs and made ourselves comfortable for the long wait. We sit in silence, only making small talk every now and then. At some point we took a catnap and woke up only to find ourselves still waiting. A couple of hours later, we are finally in the recovery room with Rodney. Déjà vu. There are tears in my eyes. I lean over and brush his hair back with my hand. A lone tear falls from my eye down to his forehead as I kiss him. I want to tell him that I know he is tired, that I know he is strong, that I know he is a winner. Instead I just say, "I love you Suga." We sit and watch the monitors only asking questions of the nurse when there is a strange beep from a machine. After about 45 minutes, again not waking him up because it takes him a while to wake up after anesthesia, we are ushered up to his ICU room. The first room they say he will be in makes me stop in my tracks. "No! I can't. No! Please don't!" The nurse looks at me with an inquiring look and she remembers and quickly shouts to the transport team, "No not here, we have another room on the other side closer to the nursing station." I thank her very

180

quietly but with sincerity. I'm thankful that she has been on my journey several times before and remembered. The room they were going to place him in originally, was the same room that Roc had transitioned in the year before. As strong as I am. That would have more than likely broke me down.

We get him settled into his bed and all of the medical equipment is transferred. The normal question and answer is done between myself and the nurse. Unfortunately, this was probably the quickest intake because he already has so much recent information in the computer system.

I explain to the nurse that I need to show my accompaniment how to get out of the hospital in order to leave. As we walk through the hospital I am given words of encouragement that I made the right choice. To believe that I did make the right choice and was not allowing another surgery just to keep him here with me must have been a question written across my forehead. For no sooner than I thought it, the statement was made. Sometimes in life, especially when for the most part you have had to make difficult decisions, we need to be reassured. This was definitely one of those times. I have always felt good about the decisions and advocating for my boys, however, this was one of those times, I needed that encouragement.

I made my way back up to his room. Looked at him as he lay peacefully in the bed. The nurse was sitting outside his door working on her computer. She peeped in the door and asked if I needed anything and I said no thank you as I raised my cup of coffee. I made myself comfortable in my chair and decided that now was going to be the best time for me to get some type of sleep in. I drifted off to sleep not because

I was sleepy but because I was mentally and physically drained.

Upon morning, the doctors started coming in and making their rounds. Rodney was the last one, so by the time they got to his room, I was anxious to hear what they had to say. I was told basically, the surgery itself was a success in alleviating some of the pressure from his intestines. However, they felt as if Rodney may not bounce back totally from it. They would definitely keep a very close watch on him and update me accordingly. I asked the normal questions about medications, time in the ICU, etc. They were very detailed with their responses, yet left things open to accommodate change later if necessary.

Over the next week or so, there was slow progress. As each day passed, I grew more hopeful that he would pull through this. He slowly started opening his eyes and then moving his body around. He was coming out of his fog. One day I arrived mid-morning and I almost dropped my coffee as I was entering into the ICU. I could hear it. Was that what I was really hearing? I continued to walk the halls and I heard it again. Yes, that was it. It was SugaPimp's infamous laugh. It made me smile harder. As I walked closer to his room, I heard it again. Then I heard that loud scream he had that made everyone around him laugh. All I could think of at the time was the song by Tye Tribbett, "If He Did It Before; He Can Do It Again". Yes God. He most definitely did it again!

By the time I stopped outside of his door, I remained behind the curtain so he couldn't see me and said to Rodney, "What are you making all of that noise for?" Silence. I'm sure he was looking around and thinking 'that's my mama's voice'.

So then I said, "I know you hear me Rodney." Then he let it out. That giggle, that chuckle, that infectious laugh he had that comes from his belly. By the time I came around the curtain he was sitting up in the bed with his head thrown back, laughing away. I could not do anything but laugh right along with him. He was so full of joy. No matter what he had been through, he always had joy.[43]

He was so excited to see me that he started shaking and rattling the bed rails. I walked in and as I got closer he reached out to me. I had to quickly put my cup of coffee down as to not drop it or allow him to smack it out of my hand in his excitement. I grabbed him around his shoulders and gently but assertively game him the biggest hug I could. That tickled him so much that he fell back on his pillow. I inquired to the nurse about his early morning. She updated me and said he woke up about two hours before I arrived and had been bathed and sang to by the tech in the room and he had been a ball of energy since then. The attending physician had seen me walk past the nursing station and followed me into the room. He was able to give me some good news of Rodney being transferred over to the regular pediatric unit as soon as they had a bed available. It would more than likely be that afternoon since they were anticipating several discharges. That was great news. It looked as if the surgery was a huge success.

After about two hours of watching Rodney sit up, shake the bed rails and lay back down, sit up, scream and lay back down and repeat himself in his happy way, the bed on the other unit became available. We packed up and we went

---

"Rejoice in the Lord always; again I will say, Rejoice." *Philippians 4:4 (NIV)*

through the halls with him sitting up, smiling and looking all around and laughing.

By the time we got him settled in his room, he was so excited to see his familiar nurses that he laughed for a whole 30 minutes. He laughed and giggled so much until he tired himself out. He laid back on his pillow and slept like a baby for about 2 hours. During his nap I was able to meet with the team of doctors that would be caring for him. Several I was familiar with while there were also a few new to this rotation in the hospital. We went over his care plan including how they were going to start feeding him. They decided that since he had such a sensitive system and had several complications since his last surgery they were going to slow walk him through everything. They wanted to start him as before on the 5cc per hour, however, they were going to try it for 12 hours as opposed to the 6 done before. So that evening, Rodney was started on the 5cc per hour of Pedialyte.

Rodney seemed to tolerate the 5cc per hour through the first 12 hour shift. The doctors were all in agreement after examining him that they would bump him up to 10cc per hour. Not only was he tolerating it but he had some bowel sounds when they listened to his gut. This was definitely some good progress.

Over the next few days, he was increased by increments of 5cc every six hours and continued to appear to make good progress. Once the Pedialyte reached the goal of 85cc per hour, the nutritionist ordered for the staff to start him on his enteral formula through his j-tube. Since the enteral formula is a little heavier, and his body was sensitive to change, Rodney was to receive 5cc per hour of the enteral formula

184

mixed with 80cc of Pedialyte. These instructions were to run for six hours and after assessment, the enteral formula would be increased by another 5cc per hour while the Pedialyte decreased by 5cc per hour.

Once the enteral formula reached the 10cc per hour, we ran into an obstacle. Rodney's stomach was beginning to distend again. He was losing his energy level and becoming lethargic. His body was not able to handle it. Orders were changed and the ordered per hour rates for both fluids were adjusted. Another 6 hours went by and there was still no change, he wasn't responding to the decrease as all thought he would. It was decided to back off and try again the next day. Several days went by and the orders were changed yet again because he was still not tolerating the enteral formula. After the nutritionist calculated nutrition and caloric intake needs, a new order was put in place with a different enteral formula. This new calculation and formula was tried over a 24 hour period and it was found to also not help. His stomach became distended again. His energy level continued to go up and down and he started to sleep a great deal more.

Another meeting was held and the team decided to do an x-ray of his abdomen before proceeding with any other adjustments. It was after this x-ray that another team meeting was called. This meeting included all attending physicians, the nutritionist, a social worker and myself. During this meeting it was explained to me that the surgery did not cure Rodney's issues. It was only a temporary fix. He was now being diagnosed with chronic intestinal pseudo-obstruction. I was informed that Rodney was not going to be able to tolerate being fed any longer through his j-tube or his g-tube. His intestines were not accepting anything. They were giving out on him altogether.

In listening to all of the doctors give their input on what was going on, I saw what direction they were heading in. I held my breath waiting for someone to say it. I knew it was coming. I just needed to hear it. Finally, the social worker looks at me and says, "We are here to see what it is that we can do to make you and Rodney comfortable." There it was. She said it. I knew what she was saying without really being straightforward. All of the meetings. All of the new faces. The specialists. This team was gathering to tell me my son was dying. One of the doctors interrupted my thoughts and said, "We have a company we recommend to our pediatric patients. There are not many companies that handle pediatric cases, however, this one works with us in helping our families from our pediatric units with hospice." Did someone just hit me in the back of my head with a bat? Did he just say hospice? Hospice. That's the end of life or at least the end before the end of life. My eyes filled with tears. I had a knot in my throat. I felt as if someone had just kicked the breath out of me. All I could hear was 'you don't have to make a decision right now', 'we can set up a meeting with the hospice representative', 'this doesn't mean we are giving up on him'. Everyone seemed to be talking all at once. Someone pushed a tissue into my hand. I couldn't move. I couldn't even wipe my tears. I was frozen and I didn't want to move for fear of moving would just make everything that was being said real. I would have to deal with it. I would have to talk about not death, but losing another child. So I sat there. Quietly. They stopped talking. There was complete silence as the room waited for my response.

I took a deep breath and exhaled very slowly and then said, "I have to seek God in this. I have never wanted to play God or prolong anything. I have always said I would do this until he says otherwise, so can we meet again on another day with the hospice representative?" The social worker said she would make the arrangements and all agreed on meeting gain later that week.

As I make my way back to Rodney's room and walk pass certain medical staff that I know have attended to Rodney at one point or another over the last 17 years, I swear I could see sorrow, sadness or sympathy in each one of their eyes. They knew. They all knew. They either saw it coming or heard about it before I went into my meeting. Yet, they couldn't bare or were not allowed to say anything to me about it. Now, as I walk pass two of the nurses that I have known for some years, I stop and my tears begin to flow as one of them reaches out to me and pulls me in close saying, "You've been an outstanding mom. You have been here for your boys more than most parents we see come through here." The words at this point don't help but the hug sure does. I take another deep breath and say my thank you and walk toward SugaPimp's room.

As I walk inside, I notice the TV is turned down and it is quiet. He is sleeping. The tech informs me that he fell asleep right after I left to go to the meeting. I walk over to his bed and just look down at him. Peace. He exudes peace. There is a surge of emotions that come bubbling up in me. I lean over and give him a kiss. I look at the tech say, "I have to go, I need some air." I remind her of my contact info on the board, say thanks and leave. As I get to the nursing station I see his nurse and the social worker, so I inform them that I am leaving and to call me if anything changes. They assure me that they will and suggest I try and get some rest.

As I sit in my vehicle in the parking garage, I turn on the radio to help drown out the thoughts in my head. Of course, the first song I hear on my gospel station touches me to the core and I just break down. I allow myself to let it all out as I sit there. It was one of those cries that no matter how much I tried to stop, it kept coming. My tears had a purpose. I just didn't know it until I finished. Once finished, there was a calm over me. I felt cleansed. I could think clearer and I knew that the hand of God was just placed on me to guide me through what was to come.

Over the next two days, I contact my family, close friends and Rodney's school, providing all with the information I had been given. It was time for the meeting and I went to the hospital accompanied by my daughter. I knew that this was going to have to be one of those times I would need to be the stronger of the two of us. So I went into the meeting acknowledging that God was still the head of my life and His will is what was best for me.[44]

Once all of the introductions were made from the new attendees, everyone pretty much let me have the floor to ask questions. Of course, I asked, "How long does he have?" The answer was an open answer. They were not able to pinpoint a time frame because of his rare medical diagnosis and because his anatomy on the inside was slightly different (proportion wise) from most patients. The hospice representative explained how things would work at the hospice facility. I listened carefully then replied, "I don't want him at a facility. I want him to be home with us. Surrounded by familiar faces and love." I was told they could indeed arrange for that to take place. They could have a hospital bed and all needed supplies delivered to my home before he was discharged. I was also informed that there would be a doctor and a nurse to come in to my home to help

----

[44] "You need to persevere so that when you have done the will of God, you will receive what he has promised." *Hebrews 10:36 (NIV)*

in his care. Overall care, would fall on me and anyone else I chose to include in his care plan.

It was at this point, the subject of feedings came up. Since he was not able to tolerate being fed, his nutrition would come from Total Parenteral Nutrition (TPN)[45]. The hospital's nutritionist will conference with the hospice car facility's nutritionist to determine what amounts of TPN would be used for Rodney. All of his infusions will come from a mixture of all the vitamins, minerals and calories similar to what he would get if he were receiving his enteral formula or food. I was also told that I would be the one who could change, mix the vitamins and hang each TPN bag (similar to IV bags) and connect the ports/catheters in a sterile setting. Training would be provided before he was discharged to ensure that I was comfortable before taking him home. The nurse from the hospice care facility explained that she would be drawing blood at least once a week to monitor his liver enzyme levels to check for liver damage which can be brought on by long-term use of TPN. There were other questions asked and answered. Finally, I was asked if I had made the decision to take him home or send him to the facility. I said, my decision is the same as it was two days ago; he is coming home and yes I will use this hospice care facility.

Paperwork was then handed to me for informational purposes as well as to sign stating I understood everything and was in agreement with the care plan. I felt as if I were signing my life away. My daughter took this very hard, so I had to hold myself together to provide her with the strength she needed. At the end of the meeting the head physician

---

[45] TPN is a form of long-term nutritional treatment needed for patients that have severe pseudo-obstruction. TPN is administered through a PICC line that includes mediports.

informed me that later that day or tomorrow a representative from the supply company would be in Rodney's hospital room to train me on the machines (TPN machines, oxygen, et al). The meeting ended and we all left to go to our designated places.

I ventured back to Rodney's room and saw that he was sleeping. I decided to start gathering his belongings together while I waited for the designated time for my training. He slept most of the afternoon, not moving much. He was no longer receiving any type of enteral feedings or Pedialyte. He was currently only receiving fluid through the PICC line that had been inserted. Enough to keep him hydrated. Once I realized he was sleeping and I had received the word from the physicians that he could be discharged the next day, I realized I had to go home and clear his room of some of his personal items in order to have space for all of his new equipment. I explained to his nurse that this was what I needed to do and she stated, "By all means mama, whatever you have to do; we are here for you and Rodney." I kissed him on his cheek and said, "I will see you in the morning sweet pea." I left to go home to prepare for a new chapter.

Going into your child's room to remove his bed and rearrange dressers for a hospital bed can be a very emotional task. I believe to this day that the only reason I was able to get through it without breaking down was that he was coming home. No I didn't know for how long. Just the mere fact that he was coming home. There are many individuals that don't get the opportunity to say their last "I love you" or "See you later" to their loved ones. With God providing me with this opportunity was a blessing. With that in mind, I had to do this with the mindset of receiving just that….a blessing. I spent the better part of the day in his room.

Preparing for what, I did not know, but ready to take it all on just as I did 17 years prior.

The next day was the big day. Just a couple of days before Christmas of 2014. Transportation had been arranged by the hospital so I would not have to worry about trying to move him myself. Once he was loaded up on the stretcher and we passed by the nursing station to say our farewells for what would be our last time on this floor. Every time over the years, that Rodney was discharged, a nurse would always say jokingly, "Now Rodney I don't want to see you again any time soon. Take care." On this day, there were a few tears, lots of smiles and many good wishes and requests to keep them updated. It was kind of like someone moving away yet everyone wanted to stay in touch. The staff had very much become our family. They listened. Advised. Loved on. Cared for. Were scratched and beat up on and accepted it. Played with. Sang songs. Most importantly, they were touched by my angel.

Getting acclimated throughout the day with all of the new equipment also included a three hour training session with a nurse that began at 9:00 that night. This nurse was very thorough and patient as she walked me step by step through every little detail that was included in the set up and removal of all the TPN supplies and devices. She ensured that I had ample supplies and vials of vitamins, syringes, needles, even down to the gauze and a Sharps container. We worked out a schedule for his TPN to be administered that would be conducive to my sleep pattern. Rodney would be receiving TPN for 18 hours per day in order to get the proper amount of nutrition and calories he needed.

The first few days were touch and go for me. It is always a little unnerving for me to do these type of things at first. I would read and then read again each step from my instructions before I would perform the next step. I was too afraid to get it wrong. I did not want to administer anything incorrectly and have any mishaps or fatal situations on my hands. Eventually, it was second nature. Very similar to his enteral feeds, just with a sterile process.

Being as though it was Christmas, I made sure I spoke with all parties involved in his medical care to transport him on Christmas Eve. It was my family's tradition to spend that night over my daughter's house to celebrate. I wanted Rodney to be a part of it just in case he was not around for next Christmas. Both the nurse and doctor advised me of how to transport him and if those directions were followed he should not have any problems. That evening came, and to this day, I thank God for my willingness to continue on with the tradition. Even though he was sleep, propped up in his wheelchair, Rodney was able to attend our Christmas dinner. Everyone who had not seen him was able to spend some time with him

SugaPimp began to perk up some over the next week. He was having bouts of laughter while playing in his bed with a family friend daily. I believe he started looking forward to his songs that were being sung by his niece. The constantly playing music in his room was very soothing to him. His favorites were being played on his CD player. He loved Beyonce of course, (what young man doesn't). He has always been a big fan of classical music, so I would play one of his Beethoven CDs. Then there were his favorite nursery rhymes that made him stop, cock his head and listen intently while smiling.

While his spirits were up and he was smiling, arrangements were made for Rodney to participate in one of the most important events of his life. A photographer volunteered his services to come to our home and photograph Rodney in his tuxedo for his senior portraits. Even though he was wheelchair bound and we were only able to dress him from the waist up, it was an event that bought tears of joy to us all. With both my daughters and a close family friend by my side (who were there day and night with me through all of this), we dressed him in the tuxedo that was also donated by a local tuxedo rental company (God is so good)! We laughed and joked with Rodney and after about two hours were satisfied with the different poses the photographer was able to get. Now my son would be able to be in the yearbook with his senior class.

After the holiday season was over, knowing that he had made it through it and was into the first of the New Year made my heart happy. On January 9, 2015, there was a private graduation ceremony at his high school TC Williams. His teacher, had ensured, (just in case), he would not make it to his actual graduation ceremony with his class in June, that he would be able do so now. So on this day, we all bundled him up and with all of the invites sent out, we took Rodney up to his school. There we were taken to an area in the school that was not only decorated but had some of his peers, the staff from the school, his teacher, assistants, the principal, alumni and a host of family and friends. Rodney was wheeled in dressed in his red cap and gown while Pomp and Circumstance blared over the speakers. Even though he was sleep through the entire ceremony, we all enjoyed it and there was not a dry eye in the room. It was just simply beautiful. I can never stress to the wonderful staff of TC Williams what this meant to me.

By the time we got back home, Rodney was pretty tired and had a very restful remainder of the afternoon. He would wake up from time to time in the afternoon and smile then fall back to sleep.

My house was filled with so much love and support during this time. Everyone would take turns going into his room and spending time with him. Then no sooner than one person realized that someone was in his room, we all would slowly end up in there around his bed talking to him, singing, playing and loving on our SugaPimp,

The day after his graduation I saw yet another change in Rodney. When I walked into his room with his prepared TPN and ready to change his bag, I noticed he had lost a little color. He was lighter, almost a yellow hue to his face. I knew that jaundice was setting in. The first thing I thought about was his liver was failing. Knowing what I had been told and also what I had researched I knew that this could be truly happening. I asked everyone in the house were they able to see it and no one else did. However, I needed to continue on believing in what God had instilled in me years ago when he blessed me with my boys. The ability to see, accept and advocate if necessary for them. I called his nurse and told her what I was seeing.. She ensured me that I was not seeing things and she would come by later that day and draw some blood to have his enzymes tested.

As I continued on with starting new bags of Rodney's TPN, he opened his eyes. While he was awake, I initially thought he was staring into space so I began talking to him. When I leaned across him, I noticed that his eyes were moving rapidly side to side and even rolling up in the top of his head. This reminded me of when he was first born. I know when a lot of babies are born, they have yet to get control over their eye muscles and they roll in the top of their eye sockets from time to time. This is what this reminded me off. However, the rapid side to side twitching his eyes were doing was something different. I made a mental note to speak with the nurse when she came later that day. I continued on and restarted his TPN and called the girls in to his room to have them change him and his bed.

After his bed bath, they had him sitting up in the bed while they were changing the sheets. I was called into his room. They were both standing there with a look of fear on their faces. I looked at Rodney and his head was cocked to the side and his eyes were as if he were staring at the ceiling, yet they were twitching side to side again. I explained to them that I had seen that earlier and of my plan to talk to the nurse when she arrived.

Over the next few hours, we kept a close watch over him, debating whether we were seeing a neurological issue coming into play as a seizure or if he was perhaps losing his sight and he was trying hard to focus. The girls decided they wanted to play with him in an attempt to distract not only him but themselves. Once he resettled into his bed, the songs and dance began again. This seemed to perk him up and he sat up and there was that familiar scream and vocalization that we had all come to love over the years. He had a burst of energy.

Later that evening, the nurse arrived and she drew her blood from one of the ports out of his PICC line. As she was standing by his bed talking to me, Rodney's eyes started twitching and rolling again. I pointed it out to her. She stated that it could definitely be some sort of seizure or even a neurological break down. She contacted the doctor and asked if he would have time to come over here to assess Rodney. He agreed and said he would be here shortly.

While the nurse continued to do all of her paperwork and order supplies for Rodney for the next seven days, we busied ourselves with things of Rodney. The doctor soon arrived and we all went back in and gathered in Rodney's room. He examined Rodney. He was able to see what we were referring to about his eyes. The doctor said he knew of my spiritual relationship with Christ so he felt comfortable saying this to me. "It appears that Rodney is looking to the heavens. At the end of life, it has been documented and seen by many, that a person near the end of life can see and hear from those that have transitioned to the afterlife and even more." I understood what he was saying. I actually agreed with what he said. I knew it was near his time. I knew because again I had felt the hand of God on me settling me down earlier that afternoon when I first saw his color as well as the eye twitching. I asked the doctor did he know how much longer and he said he could not really pinpoint but both he and the nurse agreed after looking at all of his labs, that it would not be much longer. We talked a bit more about what to expect as he neared the end and they reminded me that their 24 hour call center would be able to page a nurse as well as the doctor at any time of the day or night. They also reminded me that if he were to go into cardiac arrest or upon his demise not to call 911 since he was in hospice. I was to call the hospice facility. After our meeting and update, they both left informing me that his medical supplies to carry him through the next seven days would be arriving tomorrow.

I called the girls back into the room after to talk to them. I wanted them to be totally aware of what was going on. At this point, there was not a lot else that could be done. Just keeping him happy and clean as had been all of his life, was the best thing we could do for him now. At that moment the entire room made a pact that we would ensure that his life would continue with as much joy and laughter as possible. We rallied around him kissing, hugging, and laughing with him. Rodney waved as each of us gathered around his bed. He gave high fives and smiles. He was the picture of his life.....happy. As he laid in the hospital bed, slowly transitioning through his last days, he continued to smile. In the midst of his end, SugaPimp showed us what we saw for over 17 years. He showed us that through it all we should remain happy. In spite of the health issues and his different abilities, he smiled. It was no perfect time than at that moment for a song that captured the very essence of his being. My granddaughter decided at that point to sing to him. She sang a song called "I Wanna See You Smile" and he did just that. Bringing a heartfelt smile to each of us standing there with him.

That evening I received a call from my minister telling me that she and our Pastor wanted to come over and pray over Rodney the next day. I couldn't think of anything better at that time. When they arrived the next day, it was evident that his health was declining. A prayer of rededication and a prayer of protection was prayed over my son. Whenever he departed this life, he would be covered from all areas.

The next day as I entered into his room, I noticed he was sitting up by himself. The lights were on and the TV was on low. No one had been in there so he had not been up playing with anyone. I followed his eyesight to where they were focused. He was looking at the ceiling and he had a smile on his face. I moved in closer to his bed and asked him gently, "Rodney do you see the pretty lights?" Rodney answered with a soft monotone voice as if he were singing one note as if to say yessss. So then I asked him, "Rodney do you see your bruhbruh (brother)?" Again, he responded with the soft monotone voice as if he were singing yessss. I had to ask him one last question. So I asked, "Rodney is bruhbruh coming to get you?" Without a doubt, he answered, "yessss." He then smiled, not once taking his focus off the ceiling that was over the foot of his bed. My heart sank. It was so heavy. However, I couldn't stay in that place of heaviness. Knowing what I know. Standing on what I have stood on all of these years. I could not be selfish and not allow my son to do what He is being told to do. To go home to be with his beloved brother.

Over the next two days, I attempted to work a few hours just to get out of the house. However, the first day, I was able to make it through three hours and ended up home because I couldn't stop crying. I was so worried that I would not be around in the end. So I came home. The remainder of that day was pretty much like the one before. The only difference was that his oxygen needed to be turned up and I thank God for our family friend acting as quickly as she did to turn it up at the first sign of distress from him. By the time I was able to get home, he was sleeping and his breathing was so much better than what she had just described to me over the phone.

Upon looking at him I also noticed that his breaths were still labored even with the oxygen turned up. I contacted his nurse and told her what had happened earlier. She directed me to turn up the oxygen a little more. I did and that appeared to help. She also instructed me to begin administering the morphine that had been prescribed, filled and already at the house. I was to begin the dosage at the lowest dose prescribed and only on an as needed basis. She stated she would check back in with me in a few hours but if anything changed, for me to give her a call back.

As the day changed to night, I had to administer another dose of morphine to Rodney. His breathing had started to become even more labored. His nurse had changed her instructions from as needed to every six hours in addition to turning the oxygen up again to keep him from having to work so hard. The last thing I wanted was to see him struggle in the end. He had put up such a fight all his life battling and jumping over one obstacle or another that I just couldn't bear to see him have to fight as he is leaving. I wanted him to have the peace that he needed. We decided that we would take shifts sitting by his bedside in order not to have him by himself. So two of us would catnap while the third was sitting beside him.

By the next morning, I looked into his room and he was still laying there appearing to be sleep but I could see that his breathing was even more labored. We went on with cleaning him up and ensuring that his bed was clean.

By late afternoon, I started making calls to my other daughter and family members to include my aunt, uncles and a few close friends letting them know that our Rodney was in transition. He would not be here with us much longer and if anyone wanted to say goodbye to him, now would be the time.

I continued with administering the morphine to him which had now been increased to every two hours. He was getting to be very uncomfortable and the oxygen was up to the allowed limit. I sat down beside his bed and held his hand. As I watched him clinging to what I knew were his last few minutes I talked to him. I told him how much I loved and adored him. I explained to him that his brother was waiting for him and it was going to be alright. I told him how proud I was of him and that he accomplished a lot during his life time. I told him the hardest thing I ever could imagine telling a child…."I will be okay baby. It's okay for you to go to heaven and rest. I will love you forever Rodney."

I called my daughter and family friend into the room and explained to them that they needed to release him. I went on to explain that at the end of life, some people will hold on just for their loved ones. They refuse to let go because they know that their loved ones are hurting and they don't want to hurt them any further. I told them that it was time to say their goodbyes. I left the room and gave the two of them the time to do just that.

When I re-entered the room, I grabbed their hands and started to pray over my son. I thanked God for his life. I thanked God for the obstacles that he helped him over. I glorified God for choosing me to be there with him from start to finish. I prayed that his soul be protected during his journey to life everlasting. At the end of my prayer, I looked at my son Rodney and realized that he was resting eternally.

Rodney Keith Nelson, Jr. transitioned to life everlasting on January 14, 2015. I'm grateful for the joy you brought to our lives. We love and miss you SugaPimp!

MY NEW BEGINNING

Here I am. At the end of the year of 2015 and getting ready to turn 52 years old in a matter of a few months. The first time in my life I have ever been by myself for a significant period of time. Since the age of 16 I have been a mother. I have always had someone to care for, guide, and protect. I have made provisions for my offspring, corrected and love them unconditionally. I have had the responsibilities of going to a school for various band and choral programs, or a conference, a sporting event and even an IEP meeting. However, that is no longer my assignment.

God has blessed me with a new assignment. My new assignment is to look after me. I only have to prepare meals for myself. I don't have to run around and look for a piece of apparel for one of my girls to wear for a special event. I am no longer required to make a pharmacy run two and three times a week. It's only me. I am in a place where I have never been. However, I honestly don't know which direction I will go in. I have been told by many, 'it's your time now, so take care of yourself'. I think it's going to be one of the most challenging tasks I have ever encountered. I have become so accustomed to placing myself on the back burner. Going without. Sacrificing for my offspring so they may have, that I have to learn to take care of just me.

The journey that I have been on for the last 17 years with Rodney and Rodell has been one that I have had to learn to keep the faith and to know that things will get better eventually[46]. However, I also hope that my journey has helped others learn how to endure.

I tried to take a job this past summer to keep me busy, however, nothing would ever pan out. Again, look at God. He knows the plans He has for all of us. He knew that I needed to finish this book and if I were to work, it would not have been accomplished. The jobs that I know I should have received offers for, I heard nothing. He blocked it. So yet again, He has given me another reason to trust Him. With my trust in God, I was able to accomplish a task that I had never imagined doing. I wrote a book. I tried to write it over the last two years but kept getting sidetracked. However, two weeks after Rodney transitioned to heaven, the Lord spoke to me and said "Now it's time to write." So to God be the glory for all that He has done for me. Now I will wait and see what He will birth out of me from my journey. I will continue to lend my ear to hear his voice and instruction. That same small voice that has guided me through this journey.

After dedicating myself and learning a whole new language in the medical field and applying it to my life, I have so much more confidence. I now believe that there is nothing too hard for me to handle. This life experience has taught me so much more about God's love for us. How if we are patient and remain faithful, He will show up and give us just what we need. It has also taught me how to remain content in whatever state that I may be in. Whether I am employed or unemployed; with residence or homeless; or even surrounded by love or lonely. I can truly say that because of this assignment, I am a better person. Someone who does

---

[46]"Fear not, for I am with you; be not dismayed, for I am your god; I will strengthen you, I will help you, I will uphold you with my righteous right hand." *Isaiah 41:10 (NIV)*

not do things because others believe I should, but because God says it's what He wants me to do.

I know that I have an abundance of opportunities ahead of me that I will be able to use and bless God in the midst of. As I venture out on my own, I will continue to be there for others the best way I can, in hopes that I can help them to understand the goodness of God's grace and mercy. During this new transition for me, I ask that if Rodney (SugaPimp), Rodell (RadioRoc) or I have touched your life in any way at all, pay it forward and help someone else by bringing some happiness and love to their life. That is what my boys did for me. In spite of, they loved me and I them, unconditionally.

When you are in your darkest moments, remember that it won't last long. Any time that we go through trials and tribulations, we must remember to bless God before we see the outcome. He hears and sees all. I am a living testimony.

When it's all said and done, and I reach the end of my journey, my prayer is to be able to see those sweet boys of mine. The only way I will get to see them again, is if I continue to live a God-filled life to the best of my ability. What God has blessed me with thus far and the idea of seeing my boys again, is enough for me to do just that.

I miss my boys each and every day. However, I am so grateful that they are resting not just side by side in the cemetery, but together eternally. I wear a piece of them with me daily. I have both of their fingerprints embedded on a silver charm as a reminder of how they not only touched my life, but held my heart in their hands. I am forever thankful that through Christ, I was able to fulfill the assignment of giving birth and raising two rare children. In keeping Him first in all that we endured, I was able to go from start to finish. Until He said otherwise. With many ups and downs, twists and turns along this journey, I had to learn to trust solely on God. I had to listen to Him. I had to have faith. So, I can proudly say that, my boys' lives led me to have more faith in God.[47]

As I move faith forward in my life, there is one goal I will keep in the forefront of my mind. When it is all said and done, I look forward to hearing "Well done my good and faithful servant....Come on in." To God be the glory![48]

---

[47] "See, I am sending an angel ahead of you to guard you along the way and to bring you to the place I have prepared. *Exodus 23:20 (NIV)*
[48] "Therefore, my dear brothers and sisters, stand firm. Let nothing move you. Always give yourselves fully to the work of the Lord, because you know that your labor in the Lord is not in vain." *1Corinthians 15:57 (NIV)*

RODELL MILES NELSON

RODNEY KEITH NELSON, JR.

To Rodney and Rodell:

I am forever grateful that I was able share you with the world. As the two of you were side by side in life and now rest side by side in your graves, I will continue to wear in your honor, your fingerprints that are side by side around my neck. Knowing that you will always be with me allows me to continue making strides as the both of you have done. You have made me a better person and I love you both for that. Thank you and remember always.....LuhLuh.

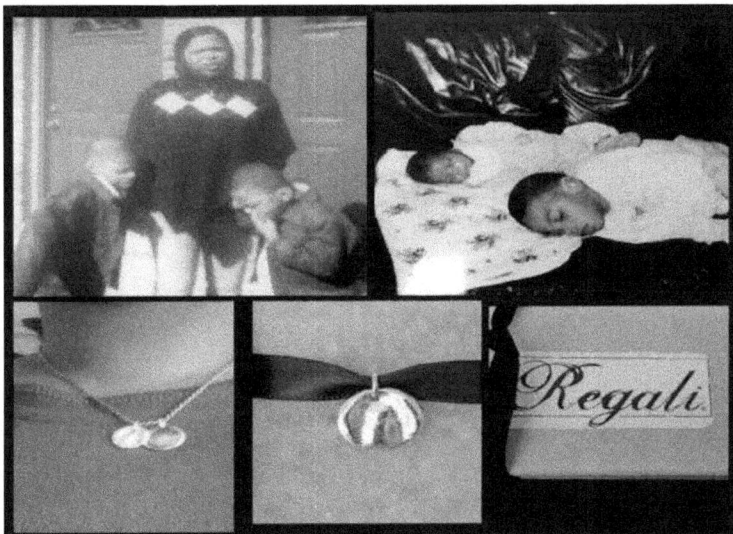

www.ingramcontent.com/pod-product-compliance
Lightning Source LLC
Chambersburg PA
CBHW060835110426